Reimagining Public

Public value theory speaks to the co-creation of value between politicians, citizens, and public managers, with a focus on the public manager in terms of her contributions, initiatives, and limitations in value creation. But just *who* are public managers? Public value regularly treats the "public manager" as synonymous with bureaucrat, government official, civil servant, or public administrator. However, the categories of public managers represent a more versatile and expansive set of agents in society than they are given credit for, and the discourse of public value has typically not delved sufficiently into the variety of possible cadres that might comprise the "public manager."

This book seeks to go beyond the assumed understandings of who the public manager is and what she does. It does so by examining the processes of value creation that are driven by *non-traditional* sets of public managers, which include the judiciary, the armed forces, multilateral institutions, and central banks. It applies public value tools to understand their value creation and uses their unique attributes to inform our understanding of public value theory. Tailored to an audience comprising public administration scholars, students of government, public officials, practitioners, and social scientists interested in contemporary problems of values in society, this book helps to advance public administration thought by re-examining the theory's ultimate protagonist: the public manager. It therefore constitutes an important effort to take public value theory forward by going "beyond" conceptions of the public manager as she has thus far been understood.

Usman W. Chohan, PhD, is a public value theorist who serves as Director for Economics and National Affairs at the Centre for Aerospace and Security Studies (CASS), and has been a post-doctoral fellow at UNSW Canberra, Australia. He has previously served at the National Bank of Canada and the World Bank. He was included among Australia's 50 Top Thinkers by the Conversation in 2016. He has resided in ten countries on five continents and is President of the International Association of Hyperpolyglots, with fluency in eight different languages. He has been a Global Shaper of the World Economic Forum and is today included among the leading business authors in the rankings of the Social Science Research Network. His most recent book, published by Routledge, is *Public Value Theory and Budgeting: International Perspectives*.

Routledge Critical Studies in Public Management
Series editor: Stephen Osborne

The study and practice of public management has undergone profound changes across the world. Over the last quarter century, we have seen

- increasing criticism of public administration as the over-arching framework for the provision of public services,
- the rise (and critical appraisal) of the 'New Public Management' as an emergent paradigm for the provision of public services,
- the transformation of the 'public sector' into the cross-sectoral provision of public services, and
- the growth of the governance of inter-organizational relationship as an essential element in the provision of public services.

In reality these trends have not so much replaced each other as elided or co-existed together – the public policy processes have not gone away as a legitimate topic of study, intra-organizational management continues to be essential to the efficient provision of public services, whilst the governance of inter-organizational and inter-sectoral relationships is now essential to the effective provision of these services.

Further, whilst the study of public management has been enriched by contribution of a range of insights from the 'mainstream' management literature, it has also contributed to this literature in such areas as networks and inter-organizational collaboration, innovation and stakeholder theory.

This series is dedicated to presenting and critiquing this important body of theory and empirical study. It will publish books that both explore and evaluate the emergent and developing nature of public administration, management and governance (in theory and practice) and examine the relationship with and contribution to the over-arching disciplines of management and organizational sociology.

Books in the series will be of interest to academics and researchers in this field, students undertaking advanced studies of it as part of their undergraduate or postgraduate degree and reflective policy makers and practitioners.

For more information about this series, please visit: www.routledge.com/Routledge-Critical-Studies-in-Public-Management/book-series/RSPM

Reimagining Public Managers
Delivering Public Value

Usman W. Chohan

LONDON AND NEW YORK

First published 2021
by Routledge
2 Park Square, Milton Park, Abingdon, Oxon OX14 4RN

and by Routledge
52 Vanderbilt Avenue, New York, NY 10017

Routledge is an imprint of the Taylor & Francis Group, an informa business

© 2021 Usman W. Chohan

The right of Usman W. Chohan to be identified as author of this work has been asserted by him in accordance with sections 77 and 78 of the Copyright, Designs and Patents Act 1988.

All rights reserved. No part of this book may be reprinted or reproduced or utilised in any form or by any electronic, mechanical, or other means, now known or hereafter invented, including photocopying and recording, or in any information storage or retrieval system, without permission in writing from the publishers.

Trademark notice: Product or corporate names may be trademarks or registered trademarks, and are used only for identification and explanation without intent to infringe.

British Library Cataloguing-in-Publication Data
A catalogue record for this book is available from the British Library

Library of Congress Cataloging-in-Publication Data
Names: Chohan, Usman W., author.
Title: Reimagining public managers: delivering public value / Usman W. Chohan.
Description: Abingdon, Oxon; New York, NY: Routledge, 2021. | Series: Routledge critical studies in public management | Includes bibliographical references and index.
Identifiers: LCCN 2020014790 (print) | LCCN 2020014791 (ebook) | ISBN 9780367418595 (hardback) | ISBN 9780367816629 (ebook)
Subjects: LCSH: Public administration—United States. | United States—Officials and employees.
Classification: LCC JK421 .C55 2020 (print) | LCC JK421 (ebook) | DDC 351.73—dc23
LC record available at https://lccn.loc.gov/2020014790
LC ebook record available at https://lccn.loc.gov/2020014791

ISBN: 978-0-367-41859-5 (hbk)
ISBN: 978-0-367-81662-9 (ebk)

Typeset in Bembo
by codeMantra

To my parents, the perfect public managers:
    Naela Chohan and Musa Javed Chohan;
    who always demonstrated a value-seeking imagination
    and leadership in the service of their people.

Contents

List of illustrations ix
About the author x
Introductory quote xii
Preface xiii
Acknowledgements xv
List of acronyms and abbreviations xvii

1 Introduction 1
 The public manager as protagonist 1
 The ambiguities of PVT 3
 The aim of this book 6
 The structure of this book 8

2 The judiciary as public manager 17
 Public value and the judiciary 17
 Judicial performance 21
 The strategic triangle 26
 Judicial activism and the politics-administration dichotomy 29
 Judicial value creation 32
 Conclusion 34

3 The armed forces as public managers 40
 Introduction 40
 Defense and security as public goods 43
 Collective security and PV destruction as creation 45
 Armed forces in non-defense value creation 47
 The strategic triangle 50
  Legitimacy and recognition 51
  Operational resources 52
 Armed forces as arbiters of value 53
 Conclusion 55

4 Multilateral public managers — 61

Introduction 61
The IMF as institution of multilateral public managers 64
Who creates value for whom? 67
The strategic triangle 71
    Legitimacy: reciprocal legitimation 71
    Recognition of value: the urgent and the important 74
    Operational resources: surrender and obsolescence 76
Multilateral PV problems 78
    Leadership of a world-public 78
    Rhetoric 79
    Value destruction 81
Conclusion 82

5 Central banks as public managers — 88

Introduction 88
The value creation of central banks 90
Central bank independence and the politics-administration dichotomy 93
The arbiters of value? 98
Strategic triangle for central banks 100
    Legitimacy 101
    Recognition of value 103
    Operational resources 104
Measuring the value of value 105
The rhetoric of central banks 106
Conclusion 108

6 Conclusion: the kaleidoscope of public managers — 114

Strategic triangle approaches 116
Recent questions in public value 118
Lessons for NTMs 120
    Interplay between NTMs 120
    Macro-micro 122
    Outfield value 124
    Politics-administration dichotomy 126
Limitations 127
Reimagining the public managers 130

Index — 133

Illustrations

Figures

1.1	The scope of public managers	6
4.1	Reciprocal legitimation: multilaterals and national politicians	73
4.2	Surrender of operational resources to multilateral public managers	77
5.1	Categories of central bank value creation	91

Tables

1.1	An outline of the chapters	9
2.1	Propositions on judiciaries	18
2.2	Strategic triangle for judiciaries	26
3.1	Propositions on armed forces	41
3.2	Strategic triangle for the armed forces	50
4.1	Derived propositions for multilateral institutions	68
4.2	Strategic triangle for the multilateral institutions (IMF)	72
5.1	Propositions on central banks	89
5.2	Forms of central bank independence	94
5.3	The strategic triangle for central banks	101
6.1	Examples of interplay between NTMs	121
6.2	Macro and micro perspectives on value creation	123
6.3	Unsuccessful attempts at outfield value creation	125
6.4	Politics–administration dichotomy: assumptions for each NTM	126

Box

2.1	Judicial performance in India	24

About the author

Dr. Usman W. Chohan (b. Manhattan, New York) is a public value theorist with specializations in budgetary theory, parliamentary fiscal scrutiny, the One Belt One Road, cryptocurrencies and blockchain, and defense economics. His research has sought to push the boundary of public value theory in search of creative and innovative solutions that drive value creation processes for the public. His most recent book, *Public Value Theory and Budgeting: International Perspectives* (Routledge, 2019), also pursues the same approach toward enriching public value theory.

Dr. Chohan serves as Director for Economics and National Affairs at the Centre for Aerospace and Security Studies (CASS), which is one of the premier research institutions in Pakistan. Dr. Chohan has also been a post-doctoral fellow at UNSW Australia, where he also completed his PhD in Economics on a full scholarship, having created the world's first multidisciplinary synthesis of Independent Legislative Fiscal Institutions, using public value to arrive at the solutions to his doctoral work. Dr. Chohan has also previously studied at McGill University, Western University, and Tsinghua University, and he has been a Global Shaper of the World Economic Forum (WEF).

Dr. Chohan is ranked among the top 12 business authors and among the top 40 out of the 400,000+ academic authors in readership over the past 12 months (as of January 2020) on the Social Science Research Network (SSRN), which is the top open-access knowledge repository in the world. In 2016, Dr. Chohan was included in the "50 Standout Articles from Australia's Top Thinkers" of the Conversation (Melbourne University Press, 2016).

Dr. Chohan previously had been a consultant with the World Bank (Social Accountability, WBI), working on issues of fiscal governance reform, and specifically, the implementation of Independent Legislative Fiscal Institutions (IFIs) to help bring impartial and nonpartisan financial expertise into global governance systems. He is a Global Advisory Board Member of Economists Without Borders. Earlier on, he had served as the Special Situations Analyst in the Global Equities Team at Natcan Investment

Management, the investment arm of the National Bank of Canada. The Global Equities team had six global investment professionals including Usman and $3 billion dollars in Assets under Management (AuM).

Dr. Chohan is the serving president of the International Association of Hyperpolyglots (HYPIA), which receives individuals who speak 6+ languages fluently, and is himself fluent in seven Indo-European languages (English, Spanish, French, Portuguese, Hindi, Urdu, and Punjabi), while also conversant in various others. Given that his last six residences were in cities on five different continents: Montreal, Buenos Aires, Islamabad, Canberra, Warsaw, and Beijing, you will likely find Dr. Usman W. Chohan roaming somewhere between these six coordinates across the earth.

Introductory quote

There is a pressing need, in my judgment, to consider what I would term "public value beyond public managers." The impetus behind public value's development has been to inform a practitioner audience about their purpose in society. To go beyond practitioner engagement and to truly engage with the theory of public value requires looking at how value for the public is created beyond the agent of "public manager" as she is typically understood. This may involve examining institutions outside of the normal ambit of public manager categorization, including the judiciary, the army, the media, and multilateral institutions. I foresee substantial merit in taking public value in the direction of such agents, and thereby either reconsidering what "public manager" means, or more importantly, looking at value creation for the public in a more abstract form with a wider field of agents.

Usman W. Chohan (2019),
Public Value Theory and Budgeting: International Perspectives, pp. 140–141

Preface

The warm and positive reception toward the ideas presented in my previous book, *Public Value Theory and Budgeting: International Perspectives,* fueled the desire to continue pursuing the line of public value inquiry that has now culminated in this book. What sets this book apart from my previous work is that although it shares the ambition of reimagining public value by extending it toward new horizons, the book goes back to first principles, asking the reader to take a long step back and ask: "just who is the public manager that public value speaks of?"

The "public manager" is an idea that has, for nearly three decades, been taken for granted and treated as synonymous with "bureaucrat" or "civil servant." Meanwhile, the largest areas of civic service provision include healthcare, social protection, education, taxation, and law enforcement, which is why much public value research has drawn focus toward these sectors. This focus, in my opinion, is undue given the versatile nature of public value creation in the 21st century.

In fact, the premise of this book is that the "public manager" is an agent more versatile than given credit for in the literature. I therefore saw the need to withdraw to a perch to reconceive of the public manager's diverse manifestations. This book is then also different from my earlier work in that, rather than deploying a single (but nonetheless powerful) lens of budgeting to provide solutions to some of public value's problems, the book casts a wider net to cover a multifaceted assortment of public managers; all while discussing their differing institutional contexts, and still staying true to the public value theorizations of a public manager and her role in the value creation processes of society.

As with all rigorous academic scrutiny, it is necessary that theory inform practice, but also reciprocally that practice must inform theory. This has been my foremost consideration in pursuing public value inquiry as set out in this book. On the one hand, a reconsideration of the public manager could help to address challenges faced by the practitioners in the fields examined in this book, including questions about their roles, their anomalies and inconsistencies, and even their future development. On the other hand, the non-traditional examinations of public managers could and should shed light on the criticisms lodged against public value theory from several corners of the academy.

As it steps outside the usual guise of public value discussions to quite an extent, I have received the full gamut of responses, ranging from the polite skepticism of public value traditionalists to the excited embrace of newer and highly promising public administration scholars. I stand behind the scholarship of this book and encourage other public administration scholars to also take bolder steps to push our discipline forward. Routledge proved very helpful and encouraging in this regard, and I was and still am ever grateful to them for their timeliness in assessing my proposal and extending the advanced contract to write this book.

Brèf, it is my pleasure to have seen so many types of public managers, as well as conceptual approaches within public value theory, subsumed into a single work, and I am elated to have advanced the public value literature, however slightly, along so fundamental a point as its protagonist, the very heroine of value creation – the public manager.

Dr. Usman W. Chohan
October 25, 2019

Acknowledgements

No book is ever truly attributable to a single author, and the journey of writing a comprehensive manuscript in any academic discipline, while often crediting the efforts of individuals, is just as much of a *collective* effort to mobilize ideas and advance the boundary of intellectual inquiry. This book too would not come to fruition without the tacit and overt support of many people.

My mother and father, Naela and Musa Chohan, both deserve the first mention for their continued support throughout the writing phase. It is not coincidental that their professional lives as public managers, devoted to the service of the people, at least subliminally informed my thinking on who the ideal public manager is and what they must do to create value for the people.

The late Prof. Kerry Jacobs, my friend and doctoral supervisor, was instrumental in pointing me toward the public value discourse at a very early juncture in my doctoral enterprise. Prof. Satish Chand, my co-supervisor, played a key supportive role in having my doctoral work seen through to completion, and then helped me to continue the post-doctoral phase during which this book was prepared. Prof. Michael O'Donnell too deserves recognition both for preserving a strong research-oriented culture at UNSW Canberra and for his support in my post-doctoral enterprise. Dr. Aron P. D'Souza also merits particular mention for his lasting and strong friendship, and for continually engaging me with interesting intellectual challenges.

The utmost recognition must go to the founders and directors of the new Centre for Aerospace and Security Studies (CASS), in Islamabad, Pakistan, including: A.C.M. Kaleem Saadat, A.V.M. Aamir Masood, Amb. Jalil Abbas Jilani, A.M. Wasim-ud-Din, A.M. Ashfaque Arain, A.V.M. Sohail Malik, A.V.M. Faheemullah Malik, Air Cdre Tanveer Piracha, and Air Cdre Adil Sultan; along with the researchers. CASS has truly come to shine in the short time since its inception, and I take pride in seeing how it has come to blossom. CASS shall rise to a great height among the research institutions of the world, *inshallah*.

There is, of course, no greater share of my gratitude than is to be attributed to *puciwuci* Joanna Koper without whom *mój mózg jest na wakacjach*. Dziękuję za wszystko, kochanie.

I am also grateful to Routledge for the excellent manner in which every phase of this book project has been managed. I hope this book is but one of many future collaborations.

Acronyms and abbreviations

ADFA	Australian Defense Forces Academy
AIIB	Asian Infrastructure Investment Bank
AJPA	Australian Journal of Public Administration
BIS	Bank of International Settlements
BRICS	Brazil, Russia, India, China, South Africa
CBI	Central Bank Independence
CBO	Congressional Budget Office (US)
CENTO	Central Treaty Organization
CEPEJ	European Commission for the Efficiency of Justice
DHA	Defense Housing Authority (Pakistan)
DOD	Department of Defense (US)
ECB	European Central Bank
EG	Eurogroup
EU	European Union
FATF	Financial Action Task Force
Fed	Federal Reserve (United States)
FSIC	Financial Stability Oversight Council (United States)
GAO	Government Accountability Office (United States)
GFC	Global Financial Crisis of 2008
GPS	Global Positioning Satellite
IFI	Independent Fiscal Institution
IJPA	International Journal of Public Administration
IMF	International Monetary Fund
JF-17	Joint-Fighter 17 (China and Pakistan)
LBO	Legislative Budget Office
NATO	North Atlantic Treaty Organization
NGOs	Non-Governmental Organizations
NTMs	Non-Traditional Managers
OBOR	One Belt One Road
OECD	Organization of Economic Cooperation and Development
PAR	Public Administration Review
PILDAT	Pakistan Institute of Legislative Development and Training

PLA	People's Liberation Army (China)
PPP	Public–Private Partnership
PV	Public Value
PVT	Public Value Theory
QE	Quantitative Easing
SEATO	Southeast Asia Treaty Organization
SIGIR	Office of the Special Inspector-General for Iraqi Reconstruction (US)
SOE	State-Owned Enterprise
SRM	Surplus Recycling Mechanism
SWF	Sovereign Wealth Fund
UNSW	University of New South Wales (Australia)
WB	World Bank
WJP	World Justice Project
WTO	World Trade Organization

Chapter 1

Introduction

The public manager as protagonist

This chapter introduces the reader to the theoretical context in which scholars of Public Value (PV) Theory can "reimagine the public manager" as an agent who is more nuanced, more versatile, and richer than how she is traditionally understood in the PV literature. To begin, we should note that in the past three decades, Mark Moore's Public Value Theory (PVT) has come to wield considerable influence in the field of public administration over both practitioners and academics (see Moore, 1994, 1995, 2003, 2007; Moore & Khagram, 2004; Moore & Donahue, 2012). My assessment has been that PVT's success and wide dissemination is attributable to its uncanny ability to raise pertinent questions about the purpose of public managers in contemporary society (see also Prebble, 2016; Chohan & Jacobs, 2017). It has served as "an anchor and as a reprieve" (Chohan, 2019, p. 1), both for the public manager as well as for those scholars who think and theorize about her role and her work. I am not alone in holding this corpus of work in high regard; it has, after all, been hailed as the "next big thing in public management" (Talbot, 2009, p. 167), and has been lauded as "a comprehensive approach to thinking about public management and about continuous improvement in public services" (Constable et al., 2008, p. 9).

To put it briefly, PVT explores the idea that "public managers" should work in concert with other social agents, and particularly with politicians and civil society, to create value for the broader public (Moore, 1994, 1995, 2003). Moore's assertion was that public managers, as agents effectuating public administration, should be "orchestrating the processes of public policy development, often in partnership with other actors and stakeholders" (Benington & Moore, 2010, p. 4). PVT therefore encourages a notion that in mobilizing public resources and mustering a "value-seeking imagination" (Moore, 1995, p. 22), the public manager should remain cognizant of her important and proactive role in improving the livelihoods of people (see also Chohan, 2017c). Williams and Shearer aptly describe the original sentiment of PVT as one that would "help imbue public sector managers with a greater appreciation of the constraints and responsibilities within which they work" (2011, p. 1367). They also praise PVT's original motive as "an affirmation of managerial ingenuity and expertise, albeit within a binding democratic order and a finite resource base," such that the public manager's purpose "is envisaged as going beyond policy implementation to the more proactive exercising of creativity and entrepreneurialism" (Williams & Shearer, 2011, p. 1372). This sense of enterprise is a virtue tempered by a need to operate harmoniously with other social agents, so as to co-create value by mustering "a coalition of sufficient support" (Benington & Turbitt, 2007, p. 383).

Therefore, whomsoever they may be, the public sector managers could, in Moore's own words, apply public value as "a framework that helps us connect what we believe is valuable and requires public resources, with improved ways of understanding what our 'publics' value, and how we connect to them" (Moore, 1995). Yet it is at precisely this juncture that I wish to draw a pause. *Whomsoever they may be?* In phrasing it thus, a sweeping mention is swung that raises the following question: just *whom* are we referring to when we speak of this powerful agent otherwise known as "the public manager?" For the past 30 years, PVT has proceeded with the assumption that its readers almost automatically knew who these people would be, and PVT has made the tacit inference that public administration scholars have a firmly encoded understanding of who public managers are. But do they? To see how deeply this assumption roots itself within the discourse, we should recall that in his very first exposition of PVT (Moore, 1994), the founder Mark Moore did not begin with any definition of the public manager. In fact, Moore began with the "what?" rather than the "who?" (1994, p. 296), and appears to have taken it for granted that his audience was clear about who the protagonists of PVT were. Hence, in lieu of elaborating on who public managers were, he instead raised three other questions that were more pressing in his judgment: "What is the goal of public sector managers? What are they supposed to produce? And how will their performance be measured?" (1994, p. 296). But who are the "they" which Moore spoke of?

Most of the public administration scholars to whom I have informally posed the question of defining the public manager often instinctively draw upon apparently synonymous terms: bureaucrats, civil servants, public officials, along with governmental and semi-governmental employees. Moore's early works themselves engaged in such ostensibly synonymous parlance through the use of titles such as "public executive," "public sector manager," and "government managers" (1994, pp. 300–301). There is ample room to make the inference that public manager is a softer-sounding term for "bureaucrat," but one that does not carry the same sociological baggage. Yet although the terms "public manager" and "bureaucrat" seem nearly synonymous, they cannot be seen as one as the same. The study of the bureaucracy (see literature review in Poocharoen, 2013) and its agent, the bureaucrat, has been met with extensive exploration in numerous fields, including anthropology (Graeber, 2015), history (Shafritz & Hyde, 2008), organizational theory (Kamenka, 1989), economics (von Mises, 1944), public administration (Albrow, 1970), and its seminal works in sociology (Weber, 1946),

What differentiates the public manager from the traditional bureaucrat can be highlighted above all in PVT's spirit of entrepreneurialism, "value-seeking imagination" (Moore, 1995, p. 22), and leadership (see also Wallis & Gregory, 2009; Wallis, 2010). These are nobler, more dynamic, more enterprising traits that not only accord higher prestige to public managers, but also set them apart from bureaucrats as active agents in the co-creation of value (see also Chohan, 2017b, 2017c). That said, as with the term "bureaucrat," the term "public manager" also tends to evoke a certain imagery of public officials working in the typical sorts of institutions long-studied in the public administration literature (Chohan, 2018). With that in mind, the crux of my argument in writing this book is that public managers are an assortment of agents who are more diverse than they are generally given credit for, and that their value-creating activities involve a greater multiplicity of methods and forms than what has been recognized in the literature. Ignoring this, in turn, stifles the sense of creative theorization of public manager's work that initially led scholars to advance PV as a worthy discourse in public administration to begin with.

The object of this book, then, is to reexamine the "public manager," and to do so by examining a series of agents who would not quite fit in the mold of the traditional public manager as she is commonly understood or represented in the PV literature. I denominate these agents as "non-traditional managers" (NTMs) and develop a set of chapters looking at different NTMs to, on the one hand, study the unusual forms of value creation that they undertake as public managers, and on the other hand, to demonstrate how their work can inform our understanding as scholars of PVT about just who public managers might well be. This is done above all with a view to reinforcing PVT's "affirmation of managerial ingenuity and expertise," so that the public manager and her purpose are "envisaged as going beyond policy implementation to the more proactive exercising of creativity and entrepreneurialism" (Williams & Shearer, 2011, p. 1372).

The ambiguities of PVT

To proceed along this line of inquiry, it is first necessary to point out just why fuller explorations of the definition of public manager have been left wanting in the literature. This is a point best attributable, I believe, to a general sense of definitional ambiguity that pervades the PV discourse. As I have explored in a recent work (Chohan, 2019), PVT has marched onwards without providing sufficient clarity on some of its most fundamental terminology. For example, even the term "public" in public value has not been given the due exploratory effort by scholars (see also Benington, 2009; Chohan, 2019, pp. 40–60). Similarly, "public manager" is just one other such term that has undergirded PVT but which has not received a sufficient amount of scholarly attention. This is part of a broader concern in public value – one of definitional ambiguities – which has been raised time and time again. Morrell remarks that "further clarification, specification and consensus over concepts and terminology" is still wanting in the PV discourse (2009), and Stoker observes that there is a "lack of clarity of response" in terms of providing "plausible answers" to various aspects of PVT (Stoker, 2006, p. 49).

Even scholars with a disposition favorable toward PVT have deemed the presence of this yawning gap to be troublesome. For example, Williams and Shearer lament that "there remains some lack of clarity over what public value is, both as a theory and as a descriptor of specific public actions and programmes" (2011, p. 1367), and they further observe that "the public value framework does not derive from a particular research tradition and there is, as yet, little by way of empirical research to support the claims made for it" (2011, p. 1381). Prebble has categorized public value's definitions as variously belonging to storytelling, an analysis of outcomes, a management practice, a tool to make operational improvements, a means of reducing the democratic deficit, a mix of outcomes and outputs, and an aspect of a relationship but not an objective fact (2016, p. 103). Therefore, PVT is perhaps most aptly characterized either by a multiplicity of hybrid definitions (van der Waal & van Hout, 2009) or as an "umbrella concept that is still being typologized" (Alford & O'Flynn, 2009, p. 187), and it therefore needs to be "rescued from ambiguity" (Prebble, 2012, p. 392).

Part of this confusion around concepts and terminology among the scholarly community, Prebble observes, is because public value was not aimed at scholars but rather at public service practitioners (2016, p. 114), so that public managers could act as "producers of real material value" (Moore, 2014, p. 465). William and Shearer weigh the positives and negatives of this, suggesting that an advantage may lie in that "public value emerges as an approach that is rooted in everyday practice and retains a non-didactic flexibility of application," but at the same time "the risk is that public value fails to develop a secure empirical foundation and loses clarity and distinctiveness as an approach to practice" (2011, p. 1374). Other scholars have been less generous in tolerating PVT's ambiguities, decrying "the Humpty Dumpty term of public value" that is "both everywhere and nowhere" (Oakley et al., 2006, p. 2; see also Crabtree, 2004), and as a result, it is but "another vague term which seems to be a messy hybrid of [public goods, public interest, and public domain] – without any of their history or intellectual robustness" (Oakley, 2006, p. 3).

Yet there is a subtler point upon which some scholars have also keenly remarked: that the transitions between the earlier definitions and the newer ones have occurred surreptitiously across the PVT literature. Many important concepts within public value have been modified over time, but often subtly and without explicit enunciation, even by stalwarts such as its founder Moore (see analysis in Prebble, 2015, 2016). As Williams and Shearer remark, "the public value doctrine has been supplemented by newer interpretations and applications and, in the process, commentators (not least Moore himself) have reworked the themes and concepts involved" (2011, p. 1367).

To see why this definitional issue is so important and of pressing concern, it may be worth recalling the enormous success that PVT has enjoyed over the past 30 years. PVT has come to serve as a mainstay in many of the world's leading schools of government and public administration academies, not least at the Kennedy School at Harvard where it was conceived (Moore, 2003). Journals such as *Public Administration Review (PAR)*, *Australian Journal of Public Administration (AJPA)*, and the *International Journal of Public Administration (IJPA)* all regularly publish articles firmly steeped in the public value discourse, and the *IJPA* and *PAR* have in fact both produced special issues on public value (see Talbot, 2009; Prebble, 2016). Thus, the criticisms of public value's inadequate exploration of some terminology, such as the "public" or the "public manager," are in part a reflection of PVT's influence and its persuasive power, which has "lent it credence but also brought critical examination of its various facets into close scrutiny" (Chohan, 2019, p. 4; see also Talbot, 2006). In an earlier work, I had quipped that "the literature seems to be in consensus about the fact that there is yet no consensus on just what public values are" (Chohan, 2019, p. 130), and yet I insisted that it would be facile of PVT scholars to just leave it at this.

As such, in this introductory chapter, I have by now sought to highlight a gap in the PVT literature as follows: along with other definitional ambiguities, the very protagonist of PVT, the so-called "public manager" has not been sufficiently defined and theorized, particularly in terms of where the boundary lies between who is and isn't a "public manager" and how her delineation might take place. So where has public value's attention remained diverted all these years? My observation is that with respect to its considerations of public managers, PVT has not delved too deeply into the possible definitions of "public manager" because it has focused on seeking case studies of *value*, both in the sense of articulating values and creating value. The main areas of interest in publications, when categorized in terms of the services/fields considered, include the following: public health, law enforcement, education, utilities, and taxation. This makes sense given the importance of these services to society's normal function and well-being. Yet what is of real interest for the purposes of this book, as mentioned earlier, is to approach non-traditional managers (NTMs), outside of these areas of typical interest in service provision, to shed a finer light on who public managers might be.

In other words, I shall look at "public managers" outside of the traditional scope of inquiry, through non-traditional agents who represent new explorations within PVT. On the one hand, this is an infusion of novelty, but on the other hand and more importantly, it is also a test for what has been hailed as PVT's "non-didactic flexibility of application" (Williams & Shearer 2011, p. 1374). Or to put it in the language of public value, these

6 Introduction

NTMs offer "concrete managerial settings" (Meynhardt, 2009, p. 214) where public value can be examined. They should serve scholars with compelling studies to "structure thinking" about what ought to be the case, as well as to "diagnose the existing situation" (Meynhardt, 2009, p. 174). It is an exercise in imagination – an effort to re-envisage the protagonist of public value through a brighter and wider kaleidoscope. Taking public value beyond the commonly conceived public manager helps to refine Mark Moore's theory, while both enriching its analysis and broadening its scope – hence this book.

The aim of this book

For the purposes of visualization, I suggest constructing a circular diagram which indicates, by ways of degree, the adherence of social agents to the identity of the usual public manager in PVT. At the core lie the traditional forms of public managers as discussed and treated in the PV literature, including public health officials, law enforcement officials, and tax and finance officials, among others. Extending a degree outwards are non-traditional managers (NTMs), who constitute the subject of this book, including judicial officials, military officials, central bankers, and international civil servants. The degree beyond this, and the most distal from the identity of public manager, lie social agents that are most evidently not public managers, such as private corporations, political parties, and civil society organizations. Two of these, civil society and political parties, are agents in PVT that are co-creators of value along with public managers; while private corporations are not given direct treatment in PVT but can engage in value creation with public managers through specific types of arrangements such as public-private partnerships (PPPs). All of this is expressed diagrammatically in Figure 1.1.

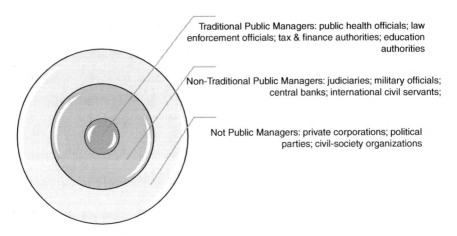

Figure 1.1 The scope of public managers.
Source: Author's research.

In this figure, domains within the core circle are scarcely disputed as being those of public managers. In fact, they comprise some of the largest and most important areas of public service provision: public health, law enforcement, taxation, and education. Much of the PVT literature uses these domains as case studies for examining PVT-related questions, particularly in the *International Journal of Public Administration*, which is the journal that treats questions of PVT most prolifically. In the outermost circle are entities that would clearly not be construed as public managers. Civil society groups and non-governmental organizations (NGOs), political parties, and private corporations could hardly be confused with public manager institutions. Yet there is a medial circle that bestrides the two, and this region is the focal point of this book.

Take the following two examples: would a senior judge or a senior military official be considered a public manager? Poocharoen responds to this question by observing that "governments define the scope and size of their bureaucracy differently; some would include the military and judiciary, while others would not" (2013, p. 333). Whether the military and judiciary, as the subjects of two chapters in this book, truly belong in the definition of public managers is therefore dependent on the country and context that we consider. They, along with the subjects of the other chapters, may loom in a space of ambiguity vis-à-vis the term "public managers," and this justifies the very pursuit of this book. Critics may correctly claim that such office-holders might not always be addressable as "public managers" in some countries, but they indeed do constitute a cadre within the formalized public administration of others. That distinction is important to make in this introductory chapter, and one that will be treated in the remainder of this book under the auspices of the following normative claim: wherever such public managers are not officially treated as formal elements of the public administration, they *should be*, at least in so far as the analysis of their public value creation activities is concerned.

Having considered the preliminary elements of PVT for the purposes of this book – its ambiguities, its tacit assumption of who public managers are, and a set of non-traditional managers who do create value but have not been addressed in PVT – I am now in a position to present the reader with a more explicit formulation of the aim of this book, as follows:

> The aim of this book is to go "beyond" public managers as they are typically understood in the PVT literature by looking at a set of non-traditional public managers in various domains. This is done with a view to deciphering their forms of value creation, such that they can inform and advance traditional understandings of value creation by public managers, and also help us reimagine who public managers might be.

This phrasing speaks to the heart of the problem as discussed throughout this introductory chapter, because given the pervasive ambiguities in PVT about even basic concepts and terminology, the theory risks befuddlement, or worse, a degree of stagnation. By looking at the agent of public manager in creative ways across new contexts, this book aims to reinvigorate public value by delving back to first principles. In examining questions about the nature of the "public manager" in a truly international context using a propositional method, I believe that this book takes an ambitious look at public managerial agency with fresh eyes across a wider horizon, and bolsters PVT's "affirmation of managerial ingenuity and expertise," so that her purpose "is envisaged as going beyond policy implementation to the more proactive exercising of creativity and entrepreneurialism" (Williams & Shearer, 2011, p. 1372).

The main research method deployed in this book, true to form in PVT (see Chohan, 2019, pp. 40–60), is propositions about public managers' value creation for each category of non-traditional manager. The propositions put forth are then substantiated by examples specific to each NTM. Although such a method falls short of addressing the critique that there is "little by way of empirical research to support the claims made for [PVT]" (Williams & Shearer, 2011, p. 1381), it offers the "judgmental latitude" (Chohan, 2019, p. 68), necessary for the "more proactive exercising of creativity and entrepreneurialism" (Williams & Shearer, 2011, p. 1372) that shapes the character of this book. The next section proceeds to elaborate on the categories of non-traditional public managers that have been chosen for deeper inquiry and why; along with (equally importantly) a consideration of how they may inform existing theoretical problems that persist in PVT (see also Alford & O'Flynn, 2009; Chohan, 2019).

The structure of this book

Although the book is divided into various chapters, this has not been done in a deliberately sequential manner, and so each of these chapters is a standalone work in its own right. Therefore, practitioners who are interested in a particular public manager type, or academics interested in a specific topic within the broader PV discourse, may wish to refer to certain chapters that address their interests. Taken together, however, the chapters help to build a portfolio of non-traditional managers that is steeped in PVT and that collectively approaches inquiry into who the public manager is in a more comprehensive manner. This novel look at the public managers, as undertaken in the later chapters of this book, is hereby presented in Table 1.1.

While this list is by no means exhaustive in terms of the possibilities of exploration of non-traditional public managers, the NTMs selected offer keen insights into (1) the versatile and multidimensional nature of the public manager, as well as into (2) broader problems that have haunted the PVT discourse. Above all, this is done with a view to "help imbue public sector managers with a greater appreciation of the constraints and responsibilities within which they work" (Williams & Shearer, 2011, p. 1367). It is worth

Table 1.1 An outline of the chapters

#	Title	Exploratory Questions	Thematic Elements	Larger Theoretical Questions in PVT
1	Introduction: Do we know the protagonist of PVT, the "public manager"? What is the degree of explicit consideration of the definition of public managers, and does this reflect a broader concern about PVT's ambiguous nature? Can the study of non-traditional managers help to bridge this gap and inform our understanding of (1) who public managers are, and (2) how they can address larger theoretical questions in PVT?			
2	The Judiciary as Public Manager	• How does the judiciary contribute to public value? • Are judges truly public managers? • What are the drivers of value creation in the judiciary?	• Judicial performance • Judicial activism • Judicial fairness	• Is PVT a greater function of the quantity of value produced or quality? • How does the third branch of government fit into PVT in terms of legitimacy, accountability, esp. when they are not bound to politicians as final arbiters of value? • How can public managers respond to the demands for value creation by the public given limited operational resources?
3	The Armed Forces as Public Managers	• How do the armed forces create value for the public? • Can the armed forces really be public managers? • What are the challenges of measuring their value? • How do the problems of public value (rhetoric, politics) arise for the armed forces?	• Defense and security as public goods • Valuation of defense • Problems of assessing citizen's values • Civil-military relations	• How do problems of public goods' measurement seep into PVT? • How are difficulties and contradictions in citizen's articulation of values reconciled by public managers? • How does the "politics-administration dichotomy" play out for institutions that can depose politicians, in terms of value measurement problems, violence, and accountability? • How does the lived experience of a public shape its values? • Can value destruction lead to value creation?

(Continued)

#	Title	Exploratory Questions	Thematic Elements	Larger Theoretical Questions in PVT
4	Multilateral Public Managers	• Who is the "public" for which multilateral institutions create "value"? • Whose "values" are reflected, and toward which "publics"? • Have multilateral institutions succeeded in creating value for an international public?	• Challenges of multilateral institutions in (1) addressing "values" and (2) creating "value" for different "publics" • Examining the field of multilateral organizations	• Who are the "final arbiters" of value in a multilateral world? • How do we determine the scope of a global public, and whose values are most vocally articulated and at the expense of whom? • How do public managers reconcile differences in values at a global level? How are operational resources diverted at this level? • What is the degree of legitimacy conferred on such institutions? What is the level of recognition for their value creation efforts? • Where are the structures of accountability for keeping a check on multilateral institutions?
5	Central Banks as Public Managers	• How do central banks create value for the public? • Do central banks address the values of citizens? • How do the dynamics of the "politics-administration dichotomy" play out in independent central banks, and what lessons can be drawn from this? • What are the impacts of de-politicizing bureaucracy in a political domain: the politics of monetary authority?	• Central bank independence • De-politicization • Central bank objectives (inflation & employment) as citizen values • The limits of monetary stimulus & bailouts • Setting the price of money as value • Accountability issues	• How does the politics-administration dichotomy play out when public managers are explicitly de-politicized? Why are such exceptions successful in contrast to the general democratic imposition of politicians over bureaucrats? • What are the trade-offs with which public managers have to contend in value creation? • What is the value of public managers who themselves determine "the value of value"? • What are the democratic implications of having unaccountable public managers at the core of the monetary system? Why might the alternative appear worse? • What is the degree of concordance between such public managers and the values articulated by citizens? • When might the very rhetoric of public managers shape the values of citizens?
6	**Conclusion & Synthesis**: The public managers of PVT are a broader category of agents than typically given credit for, and there are nuances to the legitimacy, operational resources, and recognition of their value that can be explored as a result. This breadth and versatility of public managers requires further attention, and fundamental terminology within PVT must be revisited. Further research areas are highlighted, limitations are mentioned, and concluding remarks are given on the need to take public value forward.			

providing summary justifications for each, in addition to highlighting the PV problems that they shall help to address.

Chapter 2 examines the **judiciary** through the lens of public manager. It first examines why this non-traditional institution of public managers should be studied for value creation, and then applies the lens of *judicial performance* to bifurcate the value contribution of judiciaries into "fairness" and "efficiency." This advances what the literature on judicial performance considers to be the ideal type of justice system: one that speaks to both fairness and efficiency simultaneously. The efficiency of the justice system, however, is delved into more deeply as a form of value creation in light of citizens' articulation for the provision of speedy justice as something that they value, not least in jurisdictions where a long backlog of cases exists. This will lead to a more profound question regarding PVT: is PV more so a function of the quantity of value produced or of quality? If the quality is more important, then fairness alone is sufficient in judicial emphasis. However, if quantity is more (or at least equally as) important, then high judicial performance in terms of the provision of speedy and efficient justice should represent the object of vigorous pursuit by justice systems.

Beyond this, the chapter will apply the PV framework of the strategic triangle (Moore, 1995) to the judiciary, therein raising key questions about how the third branch of government adheres to PV concepts of legitimacy, recognition, and even accountability. This is all the more intriguing when it is observed that judges as public managers are not bound or beholden to politicians as the final arbiters of value. They are (ideally) an independent branch of government, and need not "answer" to politicians in a well-functioning democracy. Finally, the chapter shall also consider how judicial public managers can or could respond to the demands for value creation by the public, given their limited operational resources. It is an almost universal observation that judiciaries are underfunded given the large and growing burden of cases that now enter courts nearly everywhere. The chapter frames this in economic terms: a function of a largely fixed supply of justice but an ever-growing demand for justice. This realization then ties back to the earlier discussion on judicial performance, and how it serves as a core element of value creation by judges as public managers.

Chapter 3 looks at the value creation of **defense forces** (militaries). As with the judiciary, Poocharoen remarks that "governments define the scope and size of their bureaucracy differently; some would include the *military* [...] while others would not" (2013, p. 333, emphasis added). Yet there are very keen lessons to be drawn by depicting military officials as public managers. Defense forces create *some* form of value, but as the economics discipline has long grudgingly remarked, their value contribution has been difficult to measure and to ascertain (Hartley, 2010, 2012). This is because defense is a *public good*, non-rivalrous and non-excludable, whose importance is held differently by every individual member of the public. Furthermore, publics that face persistent security threats ascribe value to defense expenditure differently than those that do not. The issues regarding defense as a public good help to frame the importance that military public managers might attribute to their work, but the chapter discusses inherent challenges of value creation that confront militaries, not least in the paradox that their value creation may also involve value destruction. This paradox of destruction as value creation is one that the PV literature has yet to confront.

The chapter also proceeds to situate defense forces within problems that have been pointed out in the PV literature, such as the politics-administration dichotomy (see Chohan, 2017a, p. 1009), the problems of rhetoric (Chohan & Jacobs, 2018), as well as the strategic triangle's questions about legitimacy and a recognition of public value. For example, militaries around the world can and do remove politicians from power and therefore from their position as the "final arbiters" of value (Moore, 1995, p. 38). In this sense, they can risk becoming public managers who assume the role of *arbiters* of value creation, at times detaching themselves from the articulation of values by citizens, which in its extremity can include crackdowns on civil society and the imposition of martial law. Militaries also struggle with operational resources, even in the most generous of budgetary circumstances, and so are compelled to become lean and more advanced in the provision of their value as guardians. As public managers, then, defense forces are truly unique and provide particularly rich lessons for public managers in civilian contexts as well.

Chapter 4 examines international civil servants, or **public managers at multilateral institutions** as they might otherwise be called. This chapter is thus a departure from domestic (national-level) public value creation, and looks instead at "wider notions of the public" at the international level (Chohan, 2019, p. 40; see also Benington, 2009). For context, the public managerial institution that warrants specific attention in this chapter is the International Monetary Fund (IMF). The chapter highlights how attempts to look at an aggregate international "public," which is in fact composed of many different national publics, pose a peculiar set of challenges for PV scholars. If international civil servants are public managers for a global public, then who are the "final arbiters" of value in a multilateral world? More fundamentally, what is the nature of this international "public" for which "value" is being created? Equally contentiously, the chapter asks just whose values are being reflected in multilateral institutions, toward whom are these values being directed, and at the expense of whom. This leads ominously toward questions of value destruction: do multilateral public managers become a conduit for the imposition of the values of one national public over another?

The chapter then draws upon PV's signature frameworks to ask questions about the structure of multilateral institutions of public managers, specifically through the use of the PV strategic triangle (Moore, 2003). How do public managers reconcile differences in values at a global level? How are operational resources diverted toward that end? What is the degree of legitimacy conferred on such institutions, and what is the level of recognition for their value creation efforts? Finally, where are the structures of accountability for keeping a check on multilateral institutions? These are the sorts of difficult questions that must be posed regarding the role of multilateral public managers and their institutions. The chapter thereby demonstrates how PV can become an important lens for addressing challenges that have arisen in the wake of globalization (see also Moore and Donahue, 2012; Chohan, 2019), not least in terms of the backlash that globalist institutions face today.

Chapter 5 examines **central banks** as institutions of public managers. It bifurcates the value creation of central banks into the two roles of monetary policy and financial supervision. The chapter highlights the fact that although financial supervision involves a process of co-creation with other stakeholders, central banks conduct monetary policy quite independently. In the monetary domain, they are often purposely kept de-politicized, and this raises interest from a public administration perspective because it speaks to the "politics-administration dichotomy" (Chohan, 2017a, p. 1010; see also Roberts, 1995; Chohan, 2018), as an example settled in favor of the administration instead of politics. A question then arises: why would an exception such as an independent central bank be more successful in contrast to the general democratic assumption of politicians as final arbiters of value? To answer this question through the lens of PVT, the chapter delineates how central banks create value for the public. Central banks are peculiar in this sense because they are the institution that ascribes monetary value to many (if not all) other things that citizens value. In other words, they determine the "price" of the money through which citizens then translate and contextualize a great many considerations to which they ascribe value in life. This determination of the price of money, of course, is a function of setting interest rates.

On this point, central banks also exert power over citizens and politicians through rhetoric, which is an issue of keen interest in the PV literature (see Chohan, 2017b; Chohan & Jacobs, 2018). This refers to how the statements of major central banks (e.g. the Fed in the United States) directly shape the expectations of citizens and politicians about the course of economic life. Yet central banks are not detached institutions merely imposing dictates from-on-high. Rather, they seek to address two issues in the economic realm that citizens, if not overtly then at least tacitly, consider valuable: low rates of unemployment, and low and stable rates of inflation. As such, central banks represent an intriguing group of public managers that not only take overriding decisions about addressing the values of the public, but can also proactively shape them, which is why they make an essential contribution to the inquiry of this book.

What should be gleaned from this introductory exposition into *Reimaging the Public Manager: Delivering Public Value* is that the project is ambitious in tackling multiple non-traditional forms of public managers using a propositional method to explore an international and multidimensional public managerial context. At the same time, the list of chapters is by no means a total treatment of the possibilities for inquiry into public managers that PVT offers. What it should do, however, is "help imbue public sector managers with a greater appreciation of the constraints and responsibilities within which they work," as Williams and Shearer put it (2011, p. 1367).

If anything, the research presented in this book should be seen as a stairway that future researchers should traverse toward deeper investigations into the identities of public managers. After all, it has been observed that public value needs to be "rescued from ambiguity" (Prebble, 2012, p. 392), and there is a need for "further clarification, specification and consensus over concepts and terminology" (Morrell, 2009). This book is part of that rescue effort. Public value has come a long way, but it also has a long way to go, as "neither advocates nor detractors are able to substantiate their claims with research" (Williams & Shearer, 2011, p. 1382). So in introducing the scope of this book, I hope readers will be drawn toward yet further inquiry into the public value realm and critically revisit its protagonist, the public manager, in a manner that carries the PVT discourse forward: provocatively, critically, and contemplatively.

References

Albrow, M. (1970). *Bureaucracy*. London: Pall Mall.

Alford, J., & O'Flynn, J. (2009). Making Sense of Public Value: Concepts, Critiques and Emergent Meanings. *International Journal of Public Administration, 32*(3–4), 171–191.

Benington, J. (2009). Creating the Public in Order to Create Public Value? *International Journal of Public Administration, 32*(3–4), 232–249.

Benington, J., & Moore, M. (2010). *Public Value: Theory and Practice*. Basingstoke: Palgrave MacMillan.

Benington, J., & Turbitt, I. (2007). Policing the Drumcree Demonstrations in Northern Ireland: Testing Leadership Theory in Practice. *Leadership, 3*(4), 371–395.

Chohan, U. W. (2017a). Independent Budget Offices and the Politics-Administration Dichotomy. *International Journal of Public Administration, 41*(12), 1009–1017.

Chohan, U. W. (2017b). Public Value and Bureaucratic Rhetoric. In A. Farazmand (Ed.), *Global Encyclopedia of Public Administration, Public Policy, and Governance*. Springer.

Chohan, U. W. (2017c). Public Value: Bureaucrats vs Politicians. In A. Farazmand (Ed.), *Global Encyclopedia of Public Administration, Public Policy, and Governance*. Springer.

Chohan, U. W. (2018). *The Roles of Independent Legislative Fiscal Institutions: A Multidisciplinary Approach*. (Doctoral Thesis), University of New South Wales (UNSW), Canberra.

Chohan, U. W. (2019). *Public Value and Budgeting: International Perspectives*. London: Routledge.

Chohan, U. W., & Jacobs, K. (2017). Public Value in Politics: A Legislative Budget Office Approach. *International Journal of Public Administration, 40*(12), 1063–1073. doi: 10.1080/01900692.2016.1242612

Chohan, U. W., & Jacobs, K. (2018). Public Value as Rhetoric: A Budgeting Approach. *International Journal of Public Administration, 41*(15), 1217–1227.
Constable, S., Passmore, E., & Coats, D. (2008). *Public Value and Local Accountability in the NHS*. London: NHS.
Crabtree, J. (2004). The Revolution That Started in a Library. *The New Statesman, 17*(826), 54–56.
Graeber, D. (2015). *The Utopia of Rules: On Technology, Stupidity, and the Secret Joys of Bureaucracy*. Melville House.
Hartley, K. (2010). The Case for Defence. *Defence and Peace Economics, 21*(5–6), 409–426.
Hartley, K. (2012). Conflict and Defence Output: An Economic Perspective. *Revue d'économie politique, 122*(2), 171–195.
Kamenka, E. (1989). *Bureaucracy*. Oxford: Blackwell.
Meynhardt, T. (2009). Public Value Inside: What Is Public Value Creation? *International Journal of Public Administration, 32*(3–4), 192–219.
Moore, M. (1994). Public Value as the Focus of Strategy. *Australian Journal of Public Administration, 53*(3), 296–303.
Moore, M. (1995). *Creating Public Value: Strategic Management in Government*. Cambridge, MA: Harvard University Press.
Moore, M. (2003). *The Public Value Scorecard. A Rejoinder and an Alternative to "Strategic Performance Measurement and Management in Non-Profit Organizations" by Robert Kaplan*. Hauser Center for Nonprofit Organizations Working Paper, 18.
Moore, M. (2007). Recognising Public Value: The Challenge of Measuring Performance in Government. In J. Wanna (Ed.), *A Passion for Policy: Essays in Public Sector Reform* (pp. 91–116). Canberra: Australian National University.
Moore, M. (2014). Public Value Accounting: Establishing the Philosophical Basis. *Public Administration Review, 74*(2), 465–477.
Moore, M., & Donahue, J. (2012). *Ports in a Storm: Public Management in a Turbulent World*. Cambridge, MA: Harvard University.
Moore, M., & Khagram, S. (2004). *On Creating Public Value: What Business Might Learn from Government about Strategic Management*. Cambridge: John F. Kennedy School of Government, Harvard University.
Morrell, K. (2009). Governance and the Public Good. *Public Administration, 87*(3), 538–556.
Oakley, K., Naylor, R., & Lee, D. (2006). *Giving Them What They Want: Constructing the 'Public' in Public Value*. London: BOP Consulting.
Poocharoen, O. (2013). Bureaucracy and the Policy Process. In E. F. Araral, S., M. Howlett, M. Ramesh, & X. Wu (Eds.), *Routledge Handbook of Public Policy* (pp. 349–364). Routledge.
Prebble, M. (2012). Public Value and the Ideal State: Rescuing Public Value from Ambiguity. *Australian Journal of Political Administration, 71*(4), 392–402.
Prebble, M. (2015). Public Value and the Limits to Collaboration. *International Journal of Public Administration, 38*(7), 473–485.
Prebble, M. (2016). Is "We" Singular? The Nature of Public Value. *American Review of Public Administration, 48*(2), 103–118.
Roberts, A. (1995). "Civic Discovery" as a Rhetorical Strategy. *Journal of Public Policy Analysis and Management, 14*(2), 291–307.
Shafritz, J. M., & Hyde, A. (2008). *Classics of Public Administration* (6th ed.). Boston, MA: Wadsworth.

Stoker, G. (2006). Public Value Management: A New Narrative for Networked Governance?. *American Review of Public Administration, 36*(1), 41–57.

Talbot, C. (2006). *Paradoxes and Prospects of "Public Value"*. Paper presented at the Paper presented at Tenth International Research Symposium on Public Management, Glasgow.

Talbot, C. (2009). Public Value—The Next "Big Thing" in Public Management? *International Journal of Public Administration, 32*(3–4), 167–170.

van der Waal, Z., & van Hout, E. T. (2009). Is Public Value Pluralism Paramount? The Intrinsic Multiplicity and Hybridity of Public Values. *International Journal of Public Administration Review, 32*(3–4), 220–231.

von Mises, L. (1944). *Bureaucracy*. New Haven, CT: Yale University Press.

Wallis, J. (2010). A Tale of Two Leaders: Leadership and Cultural Change at the New Zealand Treasury. *Australian Journal of Public Administration, 69*(1), 22–33.

Wallis, J., & Gregory, R. (2009). Leadership, Accountability and Public Value: Resolving a Problem in "New Governance"?. *International Journal of Public Administration, 32*(3–4), 250–273.

Weber, M. (1946). *Max Weber: Essays in Sociology*. London: Oxford University Press.

Williams, I., & Shearer, H. (2011). Appraising Public Value: Past, Present and Futures. *Public Administration, 89*(4), 1367–1384.

Chapter 2

The judiciary as public manager

Public value and the judiciary

As the first of the various chapters of this book that examine the public value creation of non-traditional public managers (NTMs), the primary aim of this chapter is to examine judiciaries through the lens of public value and situate the value creation functions of judiciaries as proactive public managers. It begins by highlighting why this institution should be studied for value creation, and then applies the lens of *judicial performance* to bifurcate the value contribution of judiciaries into "fairness" and "efficiency." In comparing both forms of value creation, the chapter aims to raise questions about the *quantity* versus the *quality* of value created by public managers. Using the toolkit of public value theory, the chapter then applies the PV framework of the *strategic triangle* (Moore, 1994, 1995) to the judiciary, specifically in terms of the triangle's nodes of legitimacy, recognition, and operational resources. This, in turn, offers the possibility of observing a unique case of public managers who enjoy either constitutional or statutory independence from politics.

As a consequence, the chapter observes that politicians are not the "final arbiters" of an independent judiciary's public value in a well-functioning democracy. An extension of this exploration is the nature of *judicial activism*, which signifies the active challenge that judiciaries pose to political structures as part of their accountability function in government, thus reinforcing discussions of the politics–administration dichotomy (Roberts, 1995). Returning to the strategic triangle, the chapter also considers how judicial public managers can respond to values articulated by the public, given their limited operational resources. Finally, the chapter insists that as a non-traditional type of public manager, judicial officials need to work toward greater fairness and efficiency simultaneously to realize fuller degrees of value creation, thus returning full circle to the examination of the two forms of value creation that judiciaries undertake. An initial enumeration of the propositions that shall be put forth is presented in Table 2.1.

Table 2.1 Propositions on judiciaries

Number	Proposition
1	The judiciary creates value for the public by delivering justice that emphasizes (1) fairness and (2) efficiency
2	Citizens value well-functioning judiciaries, and their public value is a function of both the (1) quality and (2) quantity of value produced
3	Judiciaries enjoy differing levels of legitimacy, recognition, and operational resources (nodes of the strategic triangle)
4	Judiciaries are comprised of public managers who need not defer to politicians as the "final arbiters" of value, as enshrined in their independence
5	Constraints in operational resources mitigate judicial value creation potential, and so they offer a finite supply of justice against ever-growing demands for justice.

Source: Author's research.

It should be stated at the very outset that judges or judicial officials can be seen as non-traditional public managers who co-create value along with other stakeholders through the social institutions that can collectively be called the *justice system*. The workings of justice systems derive from a long-standing and ever-evolving discipline known as *jurisprudence* (Fuller, 1969; Cotterell, 1992), which has evolved differently in diverse cultural, moral, and philosophical traditions (Fuller, 1969; Smilov, 2012). There are common thematic elements across cultures, including the provision of redress to aggrieved parties, the provision of legal frameworks or evaluation of legal rules, the fair adjudication of disputes, and the administration of speedy justice, among others (see discussions in Friedmann, 1961; Smilov, 2012; Segal, 2013). In other words, akin to the spirit of PV's multiplicity and hybridity (van der Waal & van Hout, 2009), the justice system also adheres to a multiplicity of aims and hybridity of forms (see also Segal, 2013).

There are differing levels of acceptance of judiciaries as bureaucrats (Poocharoen, 2013), as there is a diversity in the "wide range of constitutional and political systems where the judiciary enjoys certain constitutional or statutory guarantees of independence, reinforced by tradition as well as *public policy*" (Friedmann, 1961, p. 821, emphasis added). It is this reinforcement by public policy that alludes to the interplay between judiciaries and a public managerial ethos, but this, in turn, is still influenced by "jurisprudential attitudes towards judicial creativity" (Friedmann, 1961, p. 821) and reflected in a diversity of legal philosophies (see early work in Friedmann, 1961) that have sought to explain the multitude of approaches.

Various leading theories of judicial behavior – attitude theory, fact pattern theory, role theory, small group theory, organization theory, and environmental theories – tend to frame the issues of judicial behavior differently (see comprehensive reviews in Gibson, 1983), but it has been cogently argued that they only examine the underlying questions partially, and "thus, theories of judicial behavior must become more complex if they are to achieve a higher level of explanation and prediction" (Gibson, 1983, p. 7). Indeed, it has long been argued that "despite a series of very significant theoretical advances, little *cumulative* and *comprehensive theory* has been created" (Gibson, 1983, p. 8, emphasis in original). This remains true today, even as theories have increased in number and in granularity, and the assertion still rests that "the field of judicial behavior may be more balkanized today than ever before" (Gibson, 1983, p. 8).

Along with the executive and the legislature, the judiciary represents one of the three traditional branches of government. In the public administration literature's treatment of the "politics-administration dichotomy" (see Roberts, 1995; Chohan, 2017), the executive branch is usually taken to represent administration, while the legislative branch represents politics. The judiciary does not neatly fit into that dichotomy, due to the democratic arrangement known as *separation of powers* (see Segal, 2013), and judiciaries are thus occasionally thought of as the "least dangerous branch" of government (Smilov, 2012). This is in part because, although judges are clearly not politicians in the sense of seeking electoral victory or campaigning for office, judges also do not always receive the categorization of "bureaucrat" in the traditionally perceived sense (Rabkin, 1983; Poocharoen, 2013).

That said, judiciaries do have a role to play in the "administrative state" (Rabkin, 1983, p. 62), and that is the point of departure for refitting them in the mold of PV's public managers (Chohan & Jacobs, 2017a, 2017b; Chohan, 2019). On that point, however, Poocharoen remarks that "governments define the scope and size of their bureaucracy differently; some would include [the] judiciary, while others would not" (2013, p. 333). The decision to define judges as public managers is therefore culture- and context-specific. As Rabkin notes, the relationship between the judiciary and the administrative state has not always been harmonious (1983). Resistance to the establishment of public value creation programs, such as the celebrated American depression-era *New Deal*, was vociferous. President Roosevelt in fact saw the judiciary as one of the "prime barriers" to what could be recognized as value creation by traditional public managers (Rabkin, 1983, p. 62).

Judiciaries can and do pose a resistance to other branches of government in the public interest, based on their interpretations of laws, norms, statutes, and conventions; to set rulings and exert agency in accountability in the service of a wider public. In a well-functioning democracy, the judiciary is independent and thus in any case not directly beholden either to the executive or to the politicians sitting in the legislature (Rader, 1998). The judiciary does, however, undergo regular processes such as the appointment of judges to benches, which do involve the participation of the executive and legislative branches. Yet insofar as they may then be considered non-traditional public managers (NTMs), judiciaries would not consider politicians to be the "final arbiters" of their value creation in the sense that PV's founder Mark Moore initially argued (Moore, 1995, p. 38). In fact, judiciaries are themselves thought of as the most impartial of arbiters (Smilov, 2012). This point is discussed through the lens of the *politics-administration dichotomy* (Chohan, 2017) later in the chapter, and one that adds a degree of nuance to Moore's explicit theorizations, as well as their tacit implications, regarding public managers.

Before proceeding, there is an extremely important observation to make about the work of public value's founder, Mark Moore, regarding the justice system. Moore's work nominally outside the realm of public value has been closely focused on the justice system, and his writings have been very influential in criminological explorations of the shortcomings of justice provision in the United States. The prominent works in this regard include the *Dangerous Offenders: The Elusive Target of Justice* (Moore et al., 1984), *Youth Violence in America* (Moore & Tonry, 1998), and *Beyond 911: A New Era for Policing* (see Sparrow et al., 1990). Although two of these books predate the inception of public value (in the mid-1990s), Moore's work on youth violence is roughly contemporaneous with PV's early theorizations. It may therefore seem somewhat peculiar that Moore treated his explorations of these two domains separately. However, my personal reading has gleaned that in several tacit ways, this extensive research on criminal justice systems has informed Moore's work on public value as well. Above all, this is suggestive in the deficiencies in administrative structures, as well as in the agency of public managers (law enforcement officials), that both literatures emphasize. The gap, as I see it, has been in drawing explicit links between the judicial process and public value creation. Although this would have been a logical and rich source of PV inquiry, I had sought to elaborate on this gap in the introductory chapter to this book by emphasizing why the explicit theorizations of *who* the public manager is had been inadvertently absent from PVT.

What this chapter allows, therefore, is for a more explicit enunciation of the basis for linkage between the judiciary (and justice system) with public value theory. The structure of the chapter is as follows. First, a discussion of fairness and efficiency, as quality and quantity of justice, is presented through the lens of judicial performance. This identifies some of the salient elements of judicial value creation. Second, Moore's strategic triangle is applied to questions of legitimacy, recognition, operational resources, and accountability. Third, the accountability, independence, and activism of judiciaries are brought into focus in examining the notion of "final arbiters" of value in PVT. Fourth, the trend of value creation, as a function of a demand-supply gap in justice provision, is used to highlight the need for proactive judicial performance in spite of the constraints that judicial public managers face. Concluding remarks follow thereafter.

Judicial performance

Benington had argued that "public value" can be seen in two ways: first, what the public values; and second, what adds value to the public sphere (2009, p. 233). There are two implicit arguments embedded in the application of this statement to the judiciary. First, that societies and individuals value fairness across cultures, and creating fairness adds value to the public sphere (see Kim & Leung, 2007). Second, that speedy justice (efficiency) is valued across cultures and that the implementation of speedy justice adds value to society. The former point of fairness speaks to the impartial adjudication, arbitration, deliberation, and meting out of justice without prejudice to the parties seeking justice (Friedmann, 1961; Fuller, 1969). Fairness may be a complex notion (Kim & Leung, 2007), but its prima facie interpretation is quite evident since "a sense of fairness" predates the human species itself and has been identified by evolutionary biologists as deep-seated in the animal kingdom as well (Brosnan & de Waal, 2014).

Along with fairness, the idea of "efficiency" in judicial value creation requires more elaboration. The Organization of Economic Cooperation and Development (OECD) identifies the *efficiency* of the justice system as consisting of timeliness, predictability of judicial decisions, and accessibility to the service of justice (Palumbo et al., 2013, p. 9). *Justice delayed is justice denied*, as the adage goes, and having a perfectly fair system but one where all decisions are made too late is still not an adequate system. The converse is also true, where a supremely unfair judiciary may mete out rapid-fire decisions day and night but ultimately cause public value destruction. Indeed, some of the most "efficient" judiciaries of the past century have included Imperial Japan (Ramseyer & Rasmusen, 2010), Rhodesia (Holleman, 1979), and Nazi Germany (Pappe, 1960), but the fairness (and morality) of these judicial institutions has been vigorously condemned since their demise. The single-point promise of the Taliban to deliver "speedy justice" as an efficient alternate judiciary might also be added to this list (Wardak & Hamidzada, 2012; Braithwaite & Gohar, 2014, p. 531).

It is thus possible to generate a first proposition of this chapter:

Proposition 1: The judiciary creates value for the public by delivering justice that emphasizes (1) fairness and (2) efficiency

Both fairness and efficiency constitute the pillars of value creation by judicial public managers, and both must therefore be given their due share of consideration. Williams and Shearer noted that Public Value Theory (PVT) should "help imbue public sector managers with a greater appreciation of the constraints and responsibilities within which they work" (2011, p. 1367). With that in mind, fairness is proximate to the *quality* of value created, where the fairer the judiciary, the higher its quality. Meanwhile, efficiency is proximate to the *quantity* of justice provided. To better contextualize the question, judicial scholars have advanced the notion of *judicial performance* (Buscaglia & Dakolias, 1999; Palumbo et al., 2013; Voigt & El Bialy, 2016). Briefly, it is the measure of a "well-functioning" judiciary that considers the provision of generally timely justice in a generally fair environment.

Various components of a justice system's structure enhance or detract from its performance, and the salient ones include: accessibility to justice; the quality and quantity of financial and human resources devoted to justice; the efficiency of the process in terms of task specialization, management of case files, and the diffusion of information technology; and the governance structure of courts, including levels of accountability, application and measurement of performance standards, and the structure of incentives for judicial officials (Palumbo et al., 2013, p. 10). These factors are also the major determinants in the "supply" of justice (to be discussed in a later section). Although judicial performance is largely thought of as a work-in-progress around the world (Buscaglia & Dakolias, 1999; Staats et al., 2005; Palumbo et al., 2013; Voigt & El Bialy, 2016), there are meaningful divergences in standards of judicial performance between developed and developing countries. As an example, the accessibility to justice, which is gauged along three dimensions: informational, geographical (physical proximity to courts), and financial (costs of litigation), is found to have been addressed considerably in terms of the informational and geographical aspects in developed countries, but not in developing countries where they remain a constant challenge. Yet, with respect to financial access, there has remained somewhat of a challenge at all levels of economic development (Palumbo et al., 2013).

A key measure of judicial performance's efficiency is the metric of average trial length. Naturally, longer trials might be indicative of poorer efficiency, although some leeway must be given for the variety and complexity of cases that are brought before the courts. Nevertheless, OECD research has cited trial length as a determinant of confidence in the overall justice system, whereby a 10% increase in trial length translates into a 2% decrease in confidence (see Palumbo et al., 2013). It is of note that trials generally tend to be a long-drawn process, the cross-country variation notwithstanding, since trial length across 16 OECD countries has been found to average about 788 days (2.2 years, see work in Voigt & El Bialy, 2016). Trial length then correlates with other elements of efficiency such as the incurred net cost of trials for plaintiffs and defendants. As an example, research has found a moderate correlation coefficient between trial length and net cost of trials to be 0.56 (excluding outliers) across the group sample of OECD countries (CEPEJ, 2018).

An important recognition in the judicial performance literature is that the conferral of *managerial responsibilities* to judges improves the performance of the judiciary (Voigt & El Bialy, 2016). In other words, the specific framing of judges as public managers improves the performance of justice delivery to the public. The primary managerial functions that have been found to contribute the most value include the following: the supervision and organization of judges in terms of office hours, case-management, presence in court, and oversight of the hearing calendar; the appointment and supervision of administrative staff and quasi-judicial officials; the delegation of accountability among judicial ranks; and administration of the budget (CEPEJ, 2018).

In consideration of judicial performance standards, it has been argued that "the regime associated with the best performance appears to be the one in which the [main] judge has broader management responsibilities," therein highlighting how a public manager outlook can indeed drive judicial performance (Palumbo et al., 2013, p. 28). A key recommendation in this regard is that of *case flow management*, which can be defined as the set of processes used by the judiciary to manage, track, and monitor the flow of cases. This has been deemed essential by evaluation authorities such as the European Commission for the Efficiency of Justice (CEPEJ) to the improvement of judicial performance (2018). Both the trial length and the case flow management elements in judicial performance are also noteworthy in that they are *quantifiable*, which lends credence to an assertion that public value is both a function of the quality and *quantity* of value created. That said, judicial researchers have lamented that "the scarcity of comparable data limits the scope of the analysis and is a major obstacle to empirical analyses of judicial systems" (Palumbo et al., 2013, p. 34). As such, although the problems of judicial performance are experienced universally (albeit to varying degrees), understanding the nature of that universality is limited by categorical data on the experience of delivering justice around the world, despite many efforts to study judicial systems independently and in the local context.

We may now posit a second proposition of this chapter, as follows:

Proposition 2: Citizens value well-functioning judiciaries, and their public value is a function of both the (1) quality and (2) quantity of value produced

To see why judicial performance is so appealing to the public, and why they might articulate their desire for generally fair and generally efficient systems, some survey data might shed light on the matter. According to the Pew Research Centre's *Global Attitudes Survey*, European Union (EU) countries consider a fair and efficient judiciary to be of categorical importance for 87% of respondents (2019). In fact, the median conceals the greater unanimity because of negative outliers (Russia, Italy, and Poland are below 72%), in what is otherwise considered a widely accepted value of judicial fairness that is shared by citizens of EU countries as disparate as Greece (95%), the United Kingdom (92%), Hungary (95%), and Sweden (95%) (see Pew Research Centre, 2019). A similar prioritization of a fair and efficient justice system can be found around the world, from North Africa (Drake, 2012), to Latin America (Staats et al., 2005), and to South Asia (Narasappa, 2016). Even the extreme case of the Taliban is indicative in that they appealed to the Afghan public on one platform and one alone: that they would create value by delivering speedy justice to the public (Wardak & Hamidzada, 2012). This has been remarked upon widely, since "insurgents like the Taliban are assisted in seizing power by filling a rule of law vacuum with speedy justice that re-established order in a way that many rural people preferred (at least initially)" (Braithwaite & Gohar, 2014, p. 531). In other words, even in the most adverse of social conditions, speedy justice can and does serve as a potently appealing platform, and one that citizens may value immensely.

A comparison between developed and developing countries should be emphasized here for two reasons: first, that the gaps between the two cohorts is becoming stark (although both cohorts face some degree of challenge in ameliorating judicial performance); and second, that public value theory itself requires expansion into developing country contexts (see Samaratunge & Wijewardena, 2009; Chohan, 2019, pp. 21–40). On this account, a very short case study of the Indian judicial system, as presented in Box 2.1, may prove indicative of the desperate need for public value creation through higher judicial performance in the developing world.

BOX 2.1: JUDICIAL PERFORMANCE IN INDIA

At present, there are immense and severe limitations of justice provision in India (Anand, 1999; Narasappa, 2016; Sen, 2018; Sangupta, 2019; World Justice Project, 2019). India ranks 68th in the world on the *Rule of Law Index* that is prepared annually by the World Justice Project ([WJP], 2019) falling three places from its previous (2018) ranking, and is marked at third place in the South Asian region. A recent and rigorous investigation of 21 High Courts in India suggested that the trial length is 1,128 days (three years and one month), a full year longer than the OECD average, but this worsens to more than six years for subordinate courts, where the procedural limitations (including operational resources, in public value parlance) are direr (Narasappa, 2016). Meanwhile, those cases that make it to the Supreme Court take 13 years on average, thereby reinforcing the adage that *justice delayed is justice denied*. Longer trial lengths can result in greater net costs for litigating parties, as suggested earlier in this chapter, which in the case of India has been found to account for 30,000 crore Indian rupees (roughly US$4 billion) in the costs that litigants collectively spend annually in India just to attend court hearings (see Sangupta, 2019).

Questions of access to justice are exemplified by the current situation of Indian judicial system, where it has been found that nearly one-third (29%) of litigants have less than a primary-school education, making it difficult for them to follow or to even understand the proceedings of judicial routine. At the same time, 45% of litigants have an annual family income of less than one lakh INR (US$1,412 per annum), putting in them squarely in the ranks of those downtrodden and weakened by economic asymmetry in dealing with the courts (Sangupta, 2019). This economic inequality affects defendants as much as the plaintiffs, since 31% of defendants in India do not get bail because they did not have money to pay for the bond (Narasappa, 2016). The culmination of such glaring deficiencies in the Indian judiciary, on account of unfairness and inefficiency alike, is that 21% of inmates spend more time in jail than their proscribed punishment. Corruption adds to the public managerial deficiencies, as India ranks 80th in the world on the *Absence of Corruption* metric as assessed in the World Justice Project's *Rule of Law Index* (WJP, 2019), whereby participants in the justice system may need to resort to non-procedural means of achieving their objectives.

In the meantime, Indian judicial public managers struggle to create value for the public, and at the High Court level hear 70 cases *per day* on average, which can stretch to 150 cases in some instances. At the Patna High Court in the state of Bihar, for example, judges have only 2.5 minutes to hear a case, and on average, judges have approximately 5–6 minutes to decide on the case (Narasappa, 2016). It has thus been remarked that "Indian courts are also in a sorry state due to huge backlog of cases pending in courts" and that "poor judicial administration also contributes to piling of cases as backlogs" (Sen, 2018, p. 112). Yet the judiciary in India has been historically underfunded (Anand, 1999) and this makes it very difficult to cope with the increasing demands for justice that accompany a growing population and complexifying socioeconomic structure, while also failing to address the aspirations of Indian citizens who articulate the desire for a fairer and more efficient justice system (Anand, 1999; Sen, 2018). Instead, India ranks 111th on the *Order & Security* metric, which considers the protection of life and property by the justice system and state more broadly; 97th on the *Civil Justice* metric, and 77th in the world on the *Criminal Justice* metric, as assessed in the World Justice Project's *Rule of Law Index* (WJP, 2019)

The public value challenges and limitations of the Indian judiciary demonstrate the grave realities of public managerial roles in the justice system. They speak to the hurdles that reflect the lived experience of citizens, who while articulating their values of fairer and more efficient justice systems, instead find an inadequate degree of value creation for the public. This allows for the application of well-understood PVT frameworks to the conditions of judiciaries more broadly, as is done in the following section.

The strategic triangle

In arguing that judiciaries make a value contribution to the public, it serves to deploy Moore's *strategic triangle* (Moore, 1994, 1995) in light of its recognition as the "central symbol" of public value (Alford and O'Flynn, 2009, p. 173). The strategic triangle is premised on three nodes: a recognition of public value, a conferral of legitimacy, and operational resources. These are contextualized to judicial public managers in Table 2.2.

First, the legitimacy of judiciaries is a matter that prima facie might appear straightforward, but should be noted for being premised on nuances and qualifications. At the face of it, judiciaries work best when they are conferred a sufficient degree of legitimacy by other branches of government and by the public, so as to act in a manner that is independent, self-sufficient, nonpartisan, and responsible (Friedmann, 1961; Fuller, 1969; Gibson, 1983; Cotterrell, 1992; Gillman, 2001). In fact, the independence of judiciaries has

Table 2.2 Strategic triangle for judiciaries

Number	Application	Examples of Assessment
Legitimacy	Judiciaries must be perceived as legitimate, independent, self-sufficient, nonpartisan, and responsible. Legitimacy is conferred not only by the public, but also from other branches of government.	The World Justice Project (WJP) measures the legitimacy and independence of judiciaries based on: Constraints on Government Powers, Absence of Corruption, and Open Government.
Recognition of value	There must be a recognition of the value that judiciaries can provide through the provision of fair and efficient justice.	The WJP measures the recognition of value created by judiciaries in areas such as the protection of Fundamental Rights, the assistance to providing Order and Security, Regulatory Enforcement, Civil Justice, and Criminal Justice.
Operation resources	Judiciaries require a host of operating capabilities & resources, including budgetary, legal, training, enforcement, case-management, and technological resources.	The OECD has examined the types of operational resources required by judiciaries, along with the variation in their provision, and the limitations of dependence or expectation for performance based on a single element.

Source: Moore (1994, 1995), World Justice Project (2019), Palumbo et al. (2013); Author's research.

long been understood as central to their effective function (see discussions in Rabkin, 1983; Rader, 1988). Yet the degree to which legitimacy is accorded in practice to judiciaries varies considerably between countries (CEPEJ, 2018; WJP, 2019). At an advanced level, judiciaries act with independence as checks on the other two branches of government and strive toward value creation through fair systems that display relatively high levels of efficiency. On the other end of the spectrum, the courts become virtual rubber-stamping offices, reined in by other poles of political power, and fail to create sufficient value for the public due to insufficient demonstration of fairness or of efficiency in justice provision (see CEPEJ, 2018; WJP, 2019). It should be noted that legitimacy or independence does not alone or automatically translate into high degrees of value creation; a country may have a relatively independent judiciary and still have a highly inefficient system with questions about its fairness (as the Indian judiciary's case study in Box 2.1 suggested).

At the same time, perceptions about the legitimacy of the judiciary may differ between different groups of the public. For example, White Americans and African Americans have contrasting perceptions about the judicial performance of the US justice system, and rightly so given the discriminatory treatment of African Americans over a prolonged historical period, which has yet to be adequately addressed in both academic research and certainly in public policy (see review in Overby et al., 2005). This, in turn, speaks to the recent scholarship in PVT regarding contrasting signals and rhetoric given by diverse subgroups within the public (Chohan & Jacobs, 2018; Chohan, 2019). Some data on public opinion may be instructive in understanding the public's perceptions on judiciaries. Recent polling data reveals that for the Supreme Court, only 38% of respondents express a "great deal" or "quite a lot" of trust, while a full 20% express "very little trust" (Gallup, 2019). This number has stayed fairly constant over the past 15 years (2004–2019), ranging between 30% and 40% for respondents who express a high degree of trust (Gallup, 2019). For contrast, it may be noted that 73% of American respondents express a "great deal" or "quite a lot" of trust in the US Military (see militaries as public managers in the next chapter) and only 8% express "very little" trust (Gallup, 2019).

Second, the public value created by judiciaries must receive due recognition by other PV stakeholders, including politicians, other branches of government, and the public at large. The WJP measures the recognition of value created by judiciaries in areas such as the protection of fundamental rights, assistance in providing order and security, the enforcement of regulations, the provision of civil justice, and the pursuit of criminal justice (2019). The failure to receive recognition for successful value creation in these domains will limit the extent to which judiciaries can make the case for effective service to the public. At its worst, this can translate into a series of destructive outcomes for the public, such as vigilante justice, extension of private power, politicization of the judiciary, and the subversion of the rule of law (Wardak & Hamidzada,

2012; Braithwaite & Gohar, 2014). As with legitimacy, the recognition of public value creation may diverge between groups within the wider public (Overby et al., 2005), which may be a reflection of selective or discriminatory public administration in the past. In addition, in the case of the US judicial system, it may also reflect the problem of "missing minority judges," in that significant but minority portions of the wider public are not just discriminated as litigants in court, but also discriminated against in their membership within public manager institutions (Chew & Kelley-Chew, 2010). PVT has yet to grapple with such issues of discriminatory value creation (and destruction) in a robust manner, and this represents a significant gap given that PVT's founder Moore himself has extensively studied domains that exemplify public managerial discriminatory praxis (most notably the criminal justice system; see Moore et al., 1984; Moore & Tonry, 1998).

Third, judiciaries require a host of operating capabilities and resources, including budgetary, legal-technical, training, enforcement, case-management, and technological resources. On funding, the OECD has found that even developed countries spend less than 1% of their federal budgets on judiciaries, which is generally split along a 60-20-20 ratio between salaries, operating expenses, and other expenses (Palumbo et al., 2013). This budgetary constraint allows for the generalizable claim to be made that *all* judiciaries are inherently short on budgets, and this situation is only likely to worsen as the gap between the supply and demand for justice provision worsens (see details in the subsequent section). Budgetary variation is considerable between countries as well, and this weighs upon international comparisons of judicial performance. However, that said, fiscal operational resources are not the be-all-end-all of judicial performance, and previous research has shown that the link between the budget allocated to justice systems and their performance is not so clear-cut or robust, at least in OECD/developed countries (see Buscalia & Dakolias, 1999; Voigt & El Bialy, 2016).

In terms of effective investment in judicial performance, studies find that higher allocations toward transitioning to digital and information technology platforms correlate with shorter trial lengths (see Buscalia & Dakolias, 1999; Palumbo et al., 2013; Voigt & El Bialy, 2016). The impetus for a greater incorporation of technology is therefore quite compelling, but its implementation is withheld, particularly in developing countries, by the lack of stronger training programs to facilitate judicial preparedness for digitization (WJP, 2019). As the earlier case of India suggested, the fact that so many litigants are poorly literate invariably hampers their ability to follow the judicial proceedings (Narasappa, 2016), digitized or not. Technology is best co-deployed with effective case flow management procedures (see earlier section; Palumbo et al., 2013). Public managerial initiative in the judiciary would best be exemplified by the adept management of the burgeoning case load that would encompass the monitoring, oversight, delegation, scheduling, and follow-up of cases. Training judicial public managers on case flow management is therefore a priority in judicial reforms, and should comprise a key element of the training in judicial academies (CEPEJ, 2018).

We thus arrive at a third proposition:

Proposition 3: Judiciaries enjoy differing levels of legitimacy, recognition, and operational resources (nodes of the strategic triangle)

What the examination of judiciaries through the strategic triangle illustrates is that its core nodes of recognition, legitimacy, and operational resources speak directly to the experience of judiciaries in both developed and developing countries. In each instance, however, further analytical nuance is required, whether because public managerial institutions have had differentiated relationships with different groups of the wider public, or because of the need to maximize limited budgetary resources and not simply associate fiscal dispensation of judiciaries with judicial performance. The approach of the strategic triangle highlights certain forms of deficiencies in judicial public manager institutions, but it is also important to look at the converse situation, where judges can overreach their mandates and become activist institutions that challenge existing power balances or step outside the remit of their stipulated mandates (Shunmugasundaram, 2007; Sharma, 2008). This is considered in the next section.

Judicial activism and the politics-administration dichotomy

As discussed in the previous section, the independence of the judiciary from political interference is an important determinant in its structure as public managerial institution (Rader, 1988). Yet this has implications for its contextualization within the public administration literature in at least two ways: the politics-administration dichotomy (Roberts, 1995; Chohan, 2017) and the "final arbiters" of public value (Moore, 1995, p. 38). For the politics-administration dichotomy, a debate has largely centered on the notion that there is a dichotomy in the power of machinery between politicians, who are elected by a democratic process to represent the public, and public managers, who wield a technocratic expertise that allows them to execute policies. Both politicians and administration can and do work together (see Chohan & Jacobs, 2017a, 2017b), but there is nonetheless an inherent tension between the two. Judiciaries are an example of governmental architecture that is deliberately kept exempt from political interference, at least in its ideal form, because politics is perceived to meddle with the due process of law and the fairness that the justice system requires (CEPEJ, 2018; WJP, 2019; Benesh & Martinek, 2002). At the same time, legislators are by definition those who legislate new laws and oversee the implementation of old ones (their legislative and oversight functions, respectively, see Stapenhurst & Pelizzo, 2008), which means that they have an inherent interest and democratic mandate to shape the laws for the public.

In PVT, Moore had argued emphatically that in democratic dispensations, it was the politicians who were the "final arbiters" of value (Moore, 1995, p. 38). Politicians would thus take measures to respond to the values articulated by the public as part of their democratic mandate to serve as arbiters of value. And yet, when speaking of arbiters, it mustn't be forgotten that judiciaries are themselves thought of as among the most impartial of arbiters (Smilov, 2012). Furthermore, the notion of political final arbiters is itself being increasingly questioned in the PV literature (see examples in Chohan, 2019). However, for the superimposition of judiciaries onto PVT, it must be recognized that they do not need to confer the role of final arbiter to politicians in order to maximize their public value creation. In fact, they do not even need to work harmoniously with politicians, but can and should act as a check and balance on excessive political encroachment by either the executive or legislative branch (Smilov, 2012). This may involve summoning politicians to court, as well as sentencing politicians for varies degrees of breach of the law (Rabkin, 1983; Rader, 1988).

This permits a fourth proposition:

Proposition 4: Judiciaries consist of public managers who need not defer to politicians as the "final arbiters" of value, as enshrined in their independence

It has long been recognized in the PV literature that the leadership of public managerial institutions plays an immense role in the direction of the initiatives that the institutions will take (Wallis & Gregory, 2009). Yet, the fundamental issue goes beyond this to touch the nerves of a nebulous concept of "accountability" of the judiciary. As Gillman notes, judicial decision-making may be nothing more than "a sincere belief that their decision represents their best understanding of what the law requires" (Gillman, 2001, p. 486). Within the structures of the judiciary, i.e. ranging from the lower courts to the higher courts (including the Supreme Court), it has been found that there is a general level of compliance or agreement between judges at the lower courts, and decisions at higher levels are seldom overturned (Benesh & Martinek, 2002). Indeed, "overtly noncompliant decisions by Court of Appeals judges are exceedingly rare" (Segal, 2013, p. 3). The question then arises: who watches these watchmen; *quis custodiet ipsos custodes*? If judges are not accountable to politicians, as is understood to be their stance as a third pillar of government, then is there scope for judges to "overreach" their mandate? (Sharma, 2008). This question of overreach falls into an area of debate around the notion of *judicial activism* (Shunmugasundaram, 2007), and it pertains to the suggestion that judges might at times push too far against politicians or other institutional structures. However, this argument itself has been staunchly critiqued. For example, Sharma argues that "judicial overreach is a myth" which misdirects judicial focus and exaggerates the space that politicians have to interfere in judicial matters, instead misleading by suggesting that judiciaries should respect certain limits and let the politicians take over from there (Sharma, 2008, p. 15).

Two brief examples from Pakistan may warrant future research attention on judicial activism and overreach. But before doing so, it is worth mentioning that polling data from the Pakistan Institute of Legislative Development and Transparency (PILDAT) has found that respondents actually express a high degree of trust in the judiciary (2015). In fact, the judiciary is the second-most trusted institution in the country with an approval rating of 63%, second only to the military which has an approval rating of 75% (PILDAT, 2015).

The first example is of Iftikhar Chaudary, Chief Justice of Pakistan during the mid-2000s when a military government led by President (General) Musharraf was in power. Following a contest for power and the deposition of Chief Justice Chaudary by President Musharraf, a populist movement was launched by lawyers and other judicial persons to reinstate the Chief Justice (see Ahsan, 2009). This came to be known as the *Lawyer's Movement*, and having garnered sufficient public support, forced President Musharraf to step down and end a period of military rule that had by then spanned nearly a decade (Ahsan, 2009). This was the fourth (and last) time that Pakistan had come under military rule, and it was to be reverted to civilian administration by the public's support of the judiciary in challenging the status quo of power through populist as well as judicial mechanisms (a Supreme Court order; see also the next chapter on the armed forces). As such, this example would likely fall under the category of judicial activism.

A second example is that of Chief Justice Saqib Nisar, who launched a popular fundraising campaign to establish hydroelectric dams in an otherwise water-scarce country, while also proceeding to take *suo moto* notice of countless deficiencies in the public and private sector provision of services (Dagia, 2019). His "suo moto" approach was initially appreciated, and so was his dam fund initiative, to which domestic and overseas Pakistanis contributed over 9 billion PKR or US$70 million at the pre-devaluation 2019 exchange rate (Supreme Court of Pakistan, 2019). The estimated construction cost of the dam, however, was Rs. 1.4 *trillion* PKR, meaning that the fund failed to collect 99.4% of the construction requirements. Civil society groups and politicians began to question the practicality of this initiative, but Nisar threatened critics of the dam with trial for treason, while flying to overseas destinations to raise funds for the project. After the conclusion of his term, much of the dam fund remained parked in a State Bank account (Supreme Court of Pakistan, 2019), where the depreciation of the rupee, interest costs, and inflation eroded its value daily. The dam funds have remained in limbo as of this writing, and no recourse has been provided to civil society members who contributed to the dam fund but have not seen any service provision in return. Is a judge the most appropriate public manager to crowdfund civil society for contributions to a dam? This example would likely fall under the category of judicial overreach.

What the foregoing discussion should illustrate is that as public managers are deliberately made independent of political interference, judicial officials follow dynamics that are different from those of other public managers. On the one hand, they can create value without political meddling, but on the other hand, they may run the risk of judicial overreach or judicial activism. This is what PVT refers to as mustering "a coalition of sufficient support" (Benington & Turbitt, 2007, p. 383) in the public managerial exercise of value creation. That said, the notion of judicial activism and overreach are themselves contested concepts (Sharma, 2008), and the literature on jurisprudence (Gibson, 1983; Gillman, 2001), as well as practitioner examples from the developing and developed world alike, leaves room for interpretations on how and where to locate the "accountability" mechanisms for judiciaries (Rabkin, 1983), which can and do themselves act as checks and balances to other branches of government (Rader, 1988).

Judicial value creation

Do judges deploy a value-seeking imagination in the way that PV's public managers are theorized to do? (see Moore, 1995, p. 22). Gibson once observed that "judges' decisions are a function of what they prefer to do, tempered by what they think they ought to do, but constrained by what they perceive is feasible to do" (1983, p. 7). Given their operational resources, the recognition of their justice provision as value, and their legitimacy as a third and independent branch of government, judicial public managers can strive to create value for the public through provision of fair and efficient justice. The public articulates its desire for a fair society more broadly (Kim & Leung, 2007), and individuals ascribe value to justice as it is required in their normal intercourse with the public sphere. They have a demand for justice, and this must be supplied by judicial officials, which is why rudimentary supply-demand functions for justice provision can be discussed at this juncture (see also Gillman, 2001; Staats et al., 2005; Ramseyer & Rasmusen, 2010), highlighting the fact that even as the demand for justice increases, its supply remains constrained and somewhat fixed.

A fifth proposition is thus warranted, as follows:

> *Proposition 5: Constraints in operational resources mitigate judicial value creation potential, and so they offer a finite supply of justice against ever-growing demands for justice.*

The supply of justice is akin to provision of an efficient quantity of justice (judicial performance) at an expected quality (judicial fairness). This supply is premised on all three elements of the strategic triangle, but most prominently in the operational resources available to judges as public managers. Therefore, what the economists find to be *supply-side* constraints in the provision of justice (Staats et al., 2005; Ramseyer & Rasmusen, 2010), are above all the *operational resources* of public value. To provide more concrete examples, the operational resources that are found to be the largest determinants of the supply of justice include the following: the quality and quantity of financial and human resources devoted to justice; the level of efficiency in terms of task specialization, the management of case files, and the diffusion of information technology; the governance structure of courts in terms of applying and measuring performance standards; and also the structure of incentives of those providing the service of justice (Palumbo et al., 2013, p. 10). As has been discussed in earlier sections, all judiciaries face some degree of constraint (and some more than others) in their operational resources, and the backlog of justice usually means that the supply of justice is not growing or adjusting to the growth in public demand for justice.

The demand for justice, by contrast, continues to grow in societies, and there has been "a proliferation of claims against the state" (Rabkin, 1983, p. 62). The demand for justice in fact grows as a function of growth of population (a larger public) as well as the degree of complexity found in socioeconomic life (a more multifaceted and interwoven public; see Staats et al., 2005; Benington, 2009; Palumbo et al., 2013). However, the increased demand for justice also reflects the development of certain cultural traits such as litigiousness, which is also a by-product of the post-truth era (see Keyes, 2004; Higgins, 2016). Structural aspects of the economy such as the level of economic development also influence the demand for justice, with more complex economies requiring increased justice provision of various sorts (Palumbo et al., 2013); along with the general quality and quantity of legislation. Beyond this, certain internal factors are also pertinent, including costs of accessing justice, the incentivization of lawyers, the structure of legal services, the degree of certainty of the law (uniformity in interpretation), and the availability of alternative dispute-resolution mechanisms (Palumbo et al., 2013).

As such, a supply-demand gap exists and appears to grow with time due to the aforementioned factors. Judicial public managers thus face an inherent constraint in their ability to create value for public. The ability to address this widening gap differs among countries, but given the innate value of justice as articulated universally by every public due to its deep-seated evolutionary importance (Kim & Leung, 2007; Brosnan & de Waal, 2014), there is a need for judicial public managers to deploy their operational resources, seek "a coalition of sufficient support" (Benington & Turbitt, 2007, p. 383), and rely on a "value-seeking imagination" (Moore, 1995, p. 22) to provide justice in a manner that is both efficient and fair to the public.

Conclusion

The founder of public value, Mark Moore, took a deep interest in justice systems, as reflected in works such as *Dangerous Offenders: The Elusive Target of Justice* (Moore et al., 1984), *Youth Violence in America* (Moore & Tonry, 1998), and *Beyond 911: A New Era For Policing* (see Sparrow et al., 1990). While two of these books predated the inception of public value (in the mid-1990s), some of his work (e.g. youth violence) was contemporaneous with PV's early theorizations. This is why it seemed somewhat odd that (1) PVT itself did not tackle the justice system's officials as a form of public manager, and (2) these two domains were treated as separate areas of research in Moore's work. Nevertheless, a closer read might suggest that Moore's research on justice systems did influence his PVT theorizations as well, most evidently in the explorations of deficiencies in administrative structures, as well as in the agency of public managers (law enforcement officials), that both literatures emphasize. Yet an explicit link was not drawn between the two areas of inquiry: the judiciary and PVT.

This chapter has sought to bridge that longstanding gap, interpreting the judiciary as a form of non-traditional public manager (NTM) who creates value for the public through the provision of justice. The two elements that are most pressing in an analysis of "justice as public value" are, as this chapter argued, the quality and quantity of justice provided to the public. The measure of fairness reflected the quality aspect, as any judiciary worthy of the name would strive to provide impartial, balanced, and essentially fair judgments for the public's grievances. Fairness has in fact always been the priority aspect in justice systems, even at the price of extended trial procedures. However, the other element of "justice as public value" is in the efficiency of the judiciary, in terms of speedy provision of justice. This has always resided axiomatically in the proverb: *justice delayed is justice denied.*

The efficiency of the justice system incorporates the study of judicial performance, and this chapter sought to highlight important drivers of high performance. At the same time, it was noted in this chapter that fairness and efficiency were not competing priorities: both required public managerial consideration, since some of the most harshly critiqued justice systems happened to be among the most "efficient," including Nazi Germany, Imperial Japan, and Colonial Rhodesia (Pappe, 1960; Holleman, 1979; Ramseyer & Rasmusen, 2010). Meanwhile, the appeal of speedy justice was highlighted through the rather extreme example of the Taliban, in that their campaign for a coalition of sufficient public support derived from the singular promise to provide justice with immediacy (Wardak & Hamidzada, 2012; Braithwaite & Gohar, 2014, p. 531).

However, an important PV assertion in this chapter was that judiciaries face inherent limitations in the provision of fair and efficient justice, a fact that is more pronounced in developing countries, where a sizeable litany of deficiencies can be identified, and this was exemplified by the brief discussion of the Indian judiciary (see Box 2.1). The example of the Indian system was not intended to suggest that such limitations are specific to that country, since the challenges of public managers in judicial systems are much more widespread internationally, and this also reflects the need for richer study of PVT in developing country contexts (see also Samaratunge & Wijewardena, 2009). The strategic triangle helped to frame these wider problems regarding the legitimacy, recognition of value, and operational resources of judiciaries globally. A generalizable insight from the application of the strategic triangle included the realization that all judiciaries face some degree of constraint in their operational resources, even as their legitimacy and independence might be robustly enforced. However, as the discussion of this chapter also stressed, using the example of the Indian judiciary, the independence of the judiciary does not translate automatically into superior judicial performance. Another generalizable element found in the chapter was that there was a general recognition of speedy justice across publics, in part due to its inherent appeal not only to humans across cultures (Kim & Leung, 2007), but also to other species (see Brosnan & de Waal, 2014).

The treatment of the legitimacy and independence of judges raised questions about their position as arbiters of value (Smilov, 2012) distinct from politicians. PVT emphatically recognizes the democratic mandate of politicians in nominating them as the "final arbiters of value" (Moore, 1995, p. 38), but this does not cohere with the separation of judiciaries as the third branch of government, positioned in fact at times to bring legislative and executive officials to heel as a force for accountability in government. However, the PVT emphasis on accountability raised the possibility of examining judicial activism and judicial overreach as outcomes of judicial public managers attempting to create value in a manner that opposed or challenged other branches of government. At the same time, although it was acknowledged in the chapter that judicial overreach and activism are disputed concepts in the literature, two examples from Pakistan (the Lawyer's Movement and the Dam Fund) illustrated how the activities of two Chief Justices might be construed as examples of activism and overreach. This discussion helped ground the accountability concerns of PVT while revisiting the original assertion of politicians as final arbiters in PV, a point that has come to be increasingly contested in the PV literature (see Chohan, 2019).

The study of judicial officials as NTMs then led to the concern that even as their legitimacy and a recognition of their value were found to be bolstered by the public, their limited operational resources meant that there was a widening gap between the demand and the supply of justice. The supply of justice is constrained by the resources of judiciaries, but the demand for justice continues to rise due to the growth of the public itself as well as its heightened interdependency and complexity, along a set of other factors. The value ascribed to justice by the public notwithstanding, the ability to address that value thus faces inherent limitations that shall widen unless the supply of justice is made to adjust to a growing demand.

In the final analysis, the chapter has sought to highlight that as NTMs, judicial officials need to work simultaneously toward greater fairness and efficiency simultaneously to realize fuller degrees of value creation. The value for justice remains a constant across societies, but the ability of judiciaries to address the value of the public is bound by constraints. The chapter also sets the tone for further analysis of NTMs throughout the book, as public managers facing unusual structures of accountability and independence, unusual value creation capabilities, and unusual relationships and mandates toward civil society, politicians, other bureaucrats, and the public itself. Therefore, in bridging a gap between two areas of research that captivated PVT's founder Moore, the justice system, and public value, this chapter generates insights for both and adds an element of synergy to the founder's path of inquiry.

References

Ahsan, A. (2009). The Preservation of the Rule of Law in Times of Strife. *International Law, 43*(1), 73–78.

Alford, J., & O'Flynn, J. (2009). Making Sense of Public Value: Concepts, Critiques and Emergent Meanings. *International Journal of Public Administration, 32*(3–4), 171–191.

Anand, A. S. (1999). Indian Judiciary and Challenges of the 21st Century. *Indian Journal of Public Administration, 45*(3), 287–302.

Benesh, S. C., & Martinek, W. L. (2002). State Supreme Court Decision-Making in Confession Cases. *Justice System Journal, 23*(1), 109–134.

Benington, J. (2009). Creating the Public in Order to Create Public Value? *International Journal of Public Administration, 32*(3–4), 232–249.

Benington, J., & Turbitt, I. (2007). Policing the Drumcree Demonstrations in Northern Ireland: Testing Leadership Theory in Practice. *Leadership, 3*(4), 371–395.

Braithwaite, J., & Gohar, A. (2014). Restorative Justice, Policing and Insurgency: Learning from Pakistan. *Law & Society Review, 48*(3), 531–561.

Brosnan, S. F., & de Waal, F. B. (2014). Evolution of Responses to (Un) Fairness. *Science, 346*(6207), 1251–1271.

Buscaglia, E., & Dakolias, M. (1999). Comparative International Study of Court Performance Indicators. *World Bank Legal Department, Paper no.: WB20177.*

Chew, P. K., & Kelley-Chew, L. T. (2010). The Missing Minority Judges. *Journal of Gender, Race & Justice, 14*(2), 179–191.

Chohan, U. W. (2017). Independent Budget Offices and the Politics-Administration Dichotomy. *International Journal of Public Administration, 41*(12), 1009–1017.

Chohan, U. W. (2019). *Public Value and Budgeting: International Perspectives.* London: Routledge.

Chohan, U. W., & Jacobs, K. (2017a). The Presidentialisation Thesis and Parliamentary Budget Offices. *Parliamentary Affairs, 70*(2), 361–376.

Chohan, U. W., & Jacobs, K. (2017b). Public Value in Politics: A Legislative Budget Office Approach. *International Journal of Public Administration, 40*(12), 1063–1073. doi: 10.1080/01900692.2016.1242612

Chohan, U. W., & Jacobs, K. (2018). Public Value as Rhetoric: A Budgeting Approach. *International Journal of Public Administration, 41*(15), 1217–1227.
Cotterell, R. B. (1992). *The Politics of Jurisprudence: A Critical Introduction to Legal Philosophy*. Philadelphia: University of Pennsylvania Press.
Dagia, N. (2019). Justice Nisar's Legacy: Fate of the Dam Fund. *Express Tribune*.
Drake, B. (2012). *Large Majority of Egyptians Put High Priority on Fair Courts*. Washington, DC: Pew Research Centre.
European Commission for the Efficiency of Justice (CEPEJ). (2018). *CEPEJ-STAT Judicial Efficiency Database*.
Friedmann, W. (1961). Legal Philosophy and Judicial Lawmaking. *Columbia Law Review, 61*(5), 821–845.
Fuller, L. L. (1969). *The Morality of Law (Vol. 152)*. New Haven, CT: Yale University Press.
Gallup. (2019). *Confidence in Institutions*. Washington, DC: Gallup.
Gibson, J. L. (1983). From Simplicity to Complexity: The Development of Theory in the Study of Judicial Behavior. *Political Behavior, 5*(1), 7–49.
Gillman, H. (2001). What's Law Got to Do with it? Judicial Behavioralists Test the "Legal Model" of Judicial Decision-Making. *Law and Social Inquiry, 26*(3), 465–504.
Higgins, K. (2016). Post-Truth: A Guide for the Perplexed. *Nature, 540*(7631), 9–9.
Holleman, J. F. (1979). Disparities and Uncertainties in African Law and Judicial Authority: A Rhodesian Case Study. *The Journal of Legal Pluralism and Unofficial Law, 11*(17), 1–35.
Keyes, R. (2004). *The Post-Truth Era: Dishonesty and Deception in Contemporary Life*. New York: St. Martin's Press.
Kim, T. Y., & Leung, K. (2007). Forming and Reacting to Overall Fairness: A Cross-cultural Comparison. *Organizational Behavior and Human Decision Processes, 104*(1), 83–95.
Moore, M. (1994). Public Value as the Focus of Strategy. *Australian Journal of Public Administration, 53*(3), 296–303.
Moore, M. (1995). *Creating Public Value: Strategic Management in Government*. Cambridge, MA: Harvard University Press.
Moore, M. H., Estrich, S. R., McGillis, D., & Spelman, W. (1984). *Dangerous Offenders: The Elusive Target of Justice*. Cambridge, MA: Harvard University Press.
Moore, M. H., & Tonry, M. (1998). Youth Violence in America. *Crime and Justice, 24*(1), 1–26.
Narasappa, H. (2016, May 2). The Long, Expensive Road to Justice. *India Today*.
Overby, L. M., Brown, R. D., Bruce, J. M., Smith, J., C. E., & Winkle, I., J. W. (2005). Race, Political Empowerment, and Minority Perceptions of Judicial Fairness. *Social Science Quarterly, 86*(2), 444–462.
Pakistan Institute of Legislative Development and Transparency (PILDAT). (2015). *Assessment of Democracy: Pakistan*. Islamabad: PILDAT.
Palumbo, G., Giupponi, G., Nunziata, L., & Mora-Sanguinetti, J. (2013). *Judicial Performance and Its Determinants: A Cross-country Perspective*. Paris: OECD.
Pappe, H. O. (1960). On the Validity of Judicial Decisions in the Nazi Era. *Modern Law Review, 23*(2), 260–271.

Pew Research Centre Global Attitudes Survey. (2019). *Judicial Fairness, Gender Equality Seen as Very Important Priorities across Europe*. Washington, DC: Pew Research Centre.

Poocharoen, O. (2013). Bureaucracy and the Policy Process. In E. F. Araral, S., M. Howlett, M. Ramesh, & X. Wu (Eds.), *Routledge Handbook of Public Policy* (pp. 349–364). London, UK: Routledge.

Rabkin, J. (1983). The Judiciary in the Administrative State. *The Public Interest, 71*(1), 62–69.

Rader, R. R. (1988). The Independence of the Judiciary: A Critical Aspect of the Confirmation Process. *Kentucky Law Journal, 77*(4), 767–784.

Ramseyer, J. M., & Rasmusen, E. B. (2010). *Measuring Judicial Independence: The Political Economy of Judging in Japan*. Chicago, IL: University of Chicago Press.

Roberts, A. (1995). "Civic Discovery" as a Rhetorical Strategy. *Journal of Public Policy Analysis and Management, 14*(2), 291–307.

Samaratunge, R., & Wijewardena, N. (2009). The Changing Nature of Public Value in Developing Countries. *International Journal of Public Administration, 32*(3–4), 313–327.

Sangupta, A. (2019). *Independence and Accountability of the Higher Indian Judiciary*. Cambridge: Cambridge University Press.

Segal, J. (2013). Judicial Behavior. In R. Goodin (Ed.), *The Oxford Handbook of Political Science*. Oxford: Oxford University Press.

Sen, S. (2018). Indian Judiciary Imprisoned: An Integrated AHP–TOPSIS Approach to Judicial Productivity. *Global Business Review, 21*(2) 1–18.

Sharma, S. (2008). Myth of Judicial Overreach. *Economic and Political Weekly, 43*(10), 15–18.

Shunmugasundaram, R. (2007). Judicial Activism and Overreach in India. *Amicus Curiae, 72*(1), 22–28.

Smilov, D. (2012). The Judiciary: The Least Dangerous Branch? In M. Rosenfeld & A. Sajó (Eds.), *The Oxford Handbook of Comparative Constitutional Law*. Oxford: Oxford University Press.

Sparrow, M. K., Moore, M. H., & Kennedy, D. M. (1990). *Beyond 911: A New Era for Policing* (p. 105). New York: Basic Books.

Staats, J. L., Bowler, S., & Hiskey, J. T. (2005). Measuring Judicial Performance in Latin America. *Latin American Politics and Society, 47*(4), 77–106.

Stapenhurst, F., & Pelizzo, R. (2008). Tools for Legislative Oversight: An Empirical Investigation. In F. Stapenhurst, R. Pelizzo, D. Olson, & L. v. Trapp (Eds.), *Legislative Budgeting and Oversight* (pp. 9–29). Washington, DC: World Bank.

Supreme Court of Pakistan. (2019). *The Supreme Court of Pakistan and the Prime Minister of Pakistan Diamer-Bhasha and Mohmand Damns Fund*. Dam Fund Statistics Database. Islamabad: Supreme Court of Pakistan.

van der Waal, Z., & van Hout, E. T. (2009). Is Public Value Pluralism Paramount? The Intrinsic Multiplicity and Hybridity of Public Values. *International Journal of Public Administration Review, 32*(3–4), 220–231.

Voigt, S., & El-Bialy, N. (2016). Identifying the Determinants of Aggregate Judicial Performance: Taxpayers' Money Well Spent? *European Journal of Law and Economics, 41*(2), 283–319.

Wallis, J., & Gregory, R. (2009). Leadership, Accountability and Public Value: Resolving a Problem in "New Governance"? *International Journal of Public Administration, 32*(3–4), 250–273.

Wardak, A., & Hamidzada, H. (2012). The Search for Legitimate Rule, Justice and a Durable Peace: Hybrid Models of Governance in Afghanistan. *Journal of Peacebuilding & Development, 7*(2), 79–88.

Williams, I., & Shearer, H. (2011). Appraising Public Value: Past, Present and Futures. *Public Administration, 89*(4), 1367–1384.

World Justice Project. (2019). *Rule of Law Index*. Washington, DC: World Justice Project.

Chapter 3

The armed forces as public managers

Introduction

The aim of this chapter is to delve into the intriguing exercise of situating the armed forces[1] within the public managerial context of Public Value Theory (PVT). It seeks to demonstrate that there are very keen lessons to be drawn by contextualizing armed forces as non-traditional managers (NTMs) that are engaged in certain forms of public value creation. Defense forces create *some* form of value, but as the economics discipline has long grudgingly remarked, their value contribution has been difficult to measure and to ascertain (Hartley, 2010, 2012). This chapter delves into the nuances of their value provision, discussing, in turn, the nature of security as value, the articulation of citizens' value for security, value destruction in the pursuit of value preservation and creation, non-defense pursuits of value by armed forces, and the politics-administration dichotomy with the final arbiters of public value. Each of these is examined sequentially through a set of propositions. An initial enumeration of those propositions is presented in Table 3.1.

As with judiciaries examined in the previous chapter, Poocharoen remarks that "governments define the scope and size of their bureaucracy differently; some would include the military and judiciary, while others would not" (2013, p. 333). The exploration of this chapter is premised on the assertion that depicting military officials as public managers offers useful lessons for scholars of public administration more broadly and Public Value (PV) theorists more specifically. One central aspect of the question at hand is that defense is a *public good*, non-rivalrous and non-excludable, whose importance is held differently by every individual member of the public (Hartley, 2010, 2012). Furthermore, publics that face persistent security threats ascribe value to defense expenditure differently than those that do not. The issues regarding defense as a public good help to frame the importance that might be accorded to the value creation of military public managers, but the chapter discusses inherent challenges of value creation that confront militaries, not least in the paradox that their value creation may also involve value destruction. This paradox of destruction as value creation is one that the PV literature has yet to engage with.

Table 3.1 Propositions on armed forces

Number	Proposition
1	Armed forces create value by providing a public good known as "defense," which is a form of "security," and it is non-excludable and non-rivalrous.
2	Defense is valued differently by different members of the public, making it difficult to gauge the "right" level of defense provision, although publics with greater perceived security threats value defense more highly.
3	Defense is a paradoxical form of value creation because it may involve value destruction in order to preserve or assure value creation.
4	Armed forces can create value outside the realm of defense. These include innovations and spin-offs, employment, civil administrative support in crises, and even market-oriented activity.
5	Armed forces can breach the politics-administration dichotomy and become the final arbiters of value, but they risk distancing themselves from the values of their citizens

Source: Author's research.

The chapter also proceeds to situate defense forces within problems that have been pointed out in the public administration literature, such as the politics–administration dichotomy (see Roberts, 1995; Chohan, 2017, p. 1009), and Moore's strategic triangle questions about legitimacy and a recognition of public value (Moore, 1995). For example, militaries around the world can and do remove politicians from power and therefore from their position as the "final arbiters" of value (Moore, 1995, p. 38). In this sense, they can risk becoming public managers who assume the "arbitership" of value creation, and might then detach themselves from the articulation of values by citizens, which in its extremity can include crackdowns on civil society and the imposition of martial law. Militaries also struggle with operational resources, even in the most generous of budgetary circumstances, and so are compelled to become lean and more advanced in the provision of their value as guardians. As public managers, then, defense forces are truly unique and provide particularly rich lessons for public managers in civilian contexts as well, and this chapter seeks to shed a more deliberate light on those elements of public administration interest.

In his initial exploration of public value, Moore made tangential references to the military in citing how public managers engaged with politicians, arguing that "on close inspection, however, it often became clear that the professionals were defining ends as well as means. Thus, in the domain of defence policy, elected representatives knew 'how much was enough' by asking generals about the likely threats from the enemy and what was needed to meet them" (Moore, 1994, p. 298). Moore further observed that "if public managers wanted to define public value in the domain of defence policy, they consulted the generals to find out what was needed" (1994, p. 298). Unfortunately, this phrasing implied that there was a separation between military generals and the public managers, and that generals might guide public managers while not being ones themselves. Speaking to an Australian audience as an American academic (Moore, 1994), it may have seemed appropriate to do so given the sociocultural and institutional arrangement of the military within both of these societies. But is this passing remark not worth revisiting in the context of other societies where the military hierarchy could indeed be thought of as an institution of public managers? After all, as Poocharoen notes, "governments define the scope and size of their bureaucracy differently; some would include the military and judiciary, while others would not" (2013, p. 333).

In some country contexts, as this chapter shall explore, militaries would squarely fall into the category of public manager, and even into its proximate term of "bureaucrat." Even for the United States, Graeber's deep inquiry into bureaucracies in *The Utopia of Rules* (2015) remarks upon the fact that the military man was considered a form of bureaucrat initially, but that after World War 2

> the word "bureaucrat" came to attach itself almost exclusively to civil servants: even if what [military officials] do all day is sit at desks, fill out forms, and file reports, neither middle managers nor military officers are ever quite considered bureaucrats.
>
> (Graeber, 2015, p. 7)

In other words, the bureaucratic (public managerial) persona was detached from the military officer, despite the creation of value for the public by the armed forces. The introductory section of this chapter thus aims to strike at an artificial distance between civilian administration and military institutions in PVT since this implied detachment is not necessary. Moore's passing remarks about "the generals" (1994, p. 298) require a revisitation, not just because of the aspects of their value creation that have been alluded to, but also because, in the wider international context that PV aspires to engage with, the armed forces can and do serve public managerial roles; ones that in fact can inform civilian administration.

With that assertion duly made, the structure of this chapter is as follows. First, it will discuss what the economics literature recognizes is the nature of defense and security as public goods, with a view to identifying just what the value of defense forces is. Second, the chapter recognizes the legitimate use of violence, and therefore the risk of value destruction, as a possible (but not necessary) precursor to the value preservation and creation of armed forces. The paradox highlighted here is that PV destruction might also be a form of value creation, insofar as defense forces protect the public and the things that the public values through potentially destructive engagements such as open conflict. The chapter then explores some forms of value creation that armed forces accomplish outside of the traditional ambit of defense. Two areas are highlighted in particular: the series of innovations that are spin-offs from military research, and the participation of armed forces entities in both market activities and civil administration. Moore's strategic triangle is then deployed to ask questions regarding the following topics: the consistent constraints in operational resources that defense forces face; the recognition of value by the public, especially for publics that have undergone experiences of violence; as well as the issues of legitimacy of armed forces in democratic structures. This final point is given a more detailed examination through the prism of "arbiters of value," as Moore called them (1995, p. 38), whereby militaries can depose politicians and assume control of government through martial law, even as this might lead to public agitation and reactions from civil society. Finally, a concluding section seeks to bring together these points in a manner that highlights the unique nature of armed forces as public managers and the theoretical value of exploring their PV more persistently.

Defense and security as public goods

What is the public value contribution of the armed forces? The *defense economics* literature (see Chohan, 2019a) is well suited to answer this (see Engerer, 2011; Hartley, 2012), because it first notes that the provision of defense belongs to a unique class of goods that are referred to *public goods* (Bergstrom & Goodman, 1973; Hummel, 1990). Public goods are characterized by two essential traits: they are non-rivalrous and non-excludable. Non-rivalrous goods are consumed by one person without it being at the expense of another person. Non-excludable goods are provided to someone in a manner that others cannot be excluded from it. These traits can be understood through the example of air defense (see also Bergstrom & Goodman, 1973; Hummel, 1990; Hartley, 2010). First, the provision of aerial defense by an effective air force is non-rivalrous, in the sense that making the skies safe for one citizen does not automatically reduce the safety of the skies for another person (which is to say, it isn't at her expense). The provision of aerial defense by a successful air force is also non-excludable in the sense that once the skies are made safe for a city, specific citizens cannot be excluded from that safety scenario.

The provision of defense as a public good is in fact the fulfillment of a more primal need that can be called "security." In terms of a human being's basic needs, security is widely understood to represent one of the most elemental requirements for survival (see Hussein et al., 2004; Bouzenita & Boulanouar, 2016). When phrased in the negative (Baldwin, 1997), as the *avoidance of insecurity*, the concept of security can encompass numerous aspects including peace, protection, safety, insurance, and stability (Hussein et al., 2004;

Solomon et al., 2008). Security can also be framed in terms of the calculus of risk (Baldwin, 1997; Solomon et al., 2008), whereby the enhancement of security represents a mitigation of the risks that one faces. As such, in terms of the public value contribution of armed forces, the assurance of security as a fundamental need through a robust provision of defense represents a quintessential category of value (see also Cavelty & Balzacq, 2016).

This permits for the positing of a first proposition:

> *Proposition 1: Armed forces create value by providing a public good known as "defense," which is a form of "security," and it is non-excludable and non-rivalrous*

However, the value that citizens ascribe to their defense differs from person to person, since public goods create incentives for citizens, based on their non-rivalrous and non-excludable nature, to engage in freeriding behavior. Such incentives, in turn, mask the true preferences that citizens may have for such goods, and reflects what PV's founder remarked to be the problem of "a public rather than the summation of individual aspirations" (Moore, 2014, p. 469). From a PV perspective, this ambiguity creates a problem of the articulation of values, since public managers cannot determine the exact valuations that individual citizens ascribe to defense and to the preservation of a peaceful environment (Engerer, 2011). As a result, the allocation of public resources to defense is often likely to be suboptimal, representing either over- or under-expenditure, given the imprecision of the public's value for security and the divergences among members of the public on that front.

This allows for the positing of a second proposition:

> *Proposition 2: Defense is valued differently by different members of the public, making it difficult to gauge the "right" level of defense provision; although publics with greater perceived security threats value defense more highly*

Despite the ambiguities regarding the willingness to pay for defense, public managers must strive toward value creation that fulfills the basic needs of the public, including their immediate security. This is why, even in countries that do not have standing armies, there is some allocation made for law enforcement and for the protection of life and property (Hussein et al., 2004). A view of one's social media feed or of the television would suggest that there is a great deal of insecurity in the world, with some regions being more affected than others (see Cavelty & Balzacq, 2016). In places where people feel a weighty, immediate, or visceral sense of insecurity, they are likelier to prefer greater allocations of resources toward defense (Hummel, 1990; Jones-Lee, 1990; Anderton & Carter, 2009; Hartley, 2012), and will articulate this value to politicians and public managers. After all, PVT urges public managers to go beyond "narrow monetary outcomes to include that which benefits and is valued by the citizenry more generally" (Williams & Shearer, 2011, p. 1367;

see also Moore & Khagram, 2004). In that vein, economists have suggested various circuitous ways of attempting to arrive at valuations of defense spending/investment (Jones-Lee 1990; Hartley 2010; Hartley 2012), which would represent quantifying efforts to measure the public value of defense provision.

Collective security and PV destruction as creation

The notion of defense and security as public value can also be extrapolated from the national level to an international scale, where the concept of *collective security* (Kupchan, 1995; Thakur, 2016) can be applied as a form of "public value between nations" (see Chohan, 2019c, pp. 95–109). By that account, publics can pool resources together to create a set of alliances that span an interwoven defense network, and forge partnerships between the public manager institutions of their armed forces. The North Atlantic Treaty Organization (NATO) is perhaps the most well-known example of institutionalized collective security, as an attack on one nation shall be treated as an attack on all, thereby requiring all armed forces public manager institutions to mobilize against any relevant threat collectively (Kupchan, 1995). The United Nations also offers a multilateral platform for collective security (Thakur, 2016; see also multilateral public managers in the next chapter), which can include peacekeeping missions that draw upon public managers from many nationalities (Thakur, 2016; Peter, 2019).

Yet the problem of freeriding behavior in international collective security might be even more pronounced than at the national level. As an example, European NATO members have been accused of freeriding on US defense spending, which would imply that one public would derive value from the resources of another without paying their due share, but various analyses of NATO's structure contend that European Union (EU) members are in fact not freeriding if burden-sharing is considered from a more multifaceted perspective (see review in Jakobsen, 2018). At the same time, collective security is found to not always be a dependable source of assurance. As an example, Pakistan joined American alliance pacts in the Central Treaty Organization (CENTO) and Southeast Asia Treaty Organization (SEATO), both modeled on NATO, to attempt to secure alliance-based collective security (Khan, 1964). Yet when Pakistan required assistance from its allies including the United States during the War of 1971, its supposed allies were nowhere to be found (Jabeen & Mazhar, 2011). Collective security through armed forces public managers is thus a form of public value between nations that faces inherent limitations; and while it may offer a semblance of assurance during peacetime, the realities of wartime stresses may make collective security a limited or even defunct concept (see debates in Kupchan, 1995; Jabeen & Mazhar, 2011; Thakur, 2016; Peter, 2019).

In addition, it is worth noting that the realms of defense and of traditional public value are different in at least one fundamental way: the former is premised on *averting* the application of *destructive power*, or the "order of violence" as von Bredow has termed it (2018, p. 87), while the latter is generally premised on the fostering of *creative power* (see "creative power" in Hartley 2012). However, this is not to suggest that armed forces actively pursue destruction in every instance – usually their aims are to prevent or deter aggression (Thakur, 2016; Peter, 2019), and minimize threats before they arise, in an otherwise defensively postured arrangement of forces (von Bredow, 2018). At the same time, threats and risks of all sorts persist in a complex society, and their interconnectedness is heightened in an era of accelerated *hybrid warfare* (see Murray & Mansoor, 2012). The "hybrid" element of contemporary warfare includes attacks not only of conventional sorts (e.g. artillery, air power), but also of subversion in the social and economic domains (see example of the Financial Action Task Force (FATF) in Chohan, 2019b). Armed forces perform deterrent, defensive, or aggressive actions in traditional domains of security, but they alone cannot grapple with hybrid warfare, which requires a multifaceted defense that involves all elements of national power (Chohan, 2019a), including all institutions of public managers working in concert to present a credible and agile (hybrid) defense (see also Murray & Mansoor, 2012).

This permits the identification of a third proposition:

Proposition 3: Defense is a paradoxical form of value creation because it may involve value destruction in order to preserve or assure value creation

That being said, conventional forms of deterrence and violence involve the application of destructive force (Williams, 1981), and acting as public managers, the armed forces are unique in that their value creation may involve value destruction through "ordered violence" (von Bredow, 2018). They are not entirely alone in this regard, however, since other institutions such as law enforcement may also need to resort to the application of kinetic destructive force (albeit less often so and to a lesser degree) in their efforts to preserve public order or minimize criminality (Moore et al., 1984). This paradox, however, requires more rigorous PVT treatment in future research, particularly with regard to more complex or asymmetric levels of destruction (Murray & Mansoor, 2012). For example, are public managers responsible for weapons of mass destruction to justify their application beyond deterrence and rhetoric (see PVT's rhetoric in Chohan & Jacobs, 2018) toward actual use in conflict? (see Kristensen et al., 2018).

As a whole, the role of violence, both tacit and overt, with respect to public administration (and especially PVT) requires greater theorization, the excellent recent work by *critical social theorists* notwithstanding (see reviews in Box, 2003, 2015). It has been argued that this lapse in public administration inquiry is attributable to the level of focus, since violence is "largely ignored in public administration, a field in which people concentrate on micro implementation rather than macro societal context and often avoid questioning oppressive or inequitable structures and practices" (Box, 2015, p. 4). PVT has yet to substantively grapple with these questions, and that line of inquiry may take time to be infused into the PV discourse, due above all to the political undertones of PVT itself. For structural violence, given PV's accommodative implicit stance toward the "one-dimensional society," as critical theorists have put it (see Marcuse, 1964), which is to say: of domination by neoliberal market forces, PVT seeks a somewhat friendly co-existence or accommodation of the public manager within a predominately neoliberal market-centric logic. It seeks to re-emphasize the importance of public managers without ruffling the feathers of neoliberal forces themselves (Benington, 2009). As Benington keenly remarks, PVT had

> developed initially in the United States in the early to mid-1990s, at the height of the dominance of the neo-liberal ideology which privileged models based on individual consumers within a private competitive market over communal citizens within a public democratic state.
> (2009, p. 232)

This philosophical impediment, albeit a significant one, can be overcome as PVT is developed more rigorously to encompass the "multiplicity and hybridity" (van der Waal & van Hout, 2009, p. 220) of perspectives that are claimed to be pursued on its behalf. In remarking upon this gap in the study of violence and public administration, this chapter seeks to highlight the example of armed forces public managers as officials who, while aiming to maintain deterrence and peacetime conditions, may be compelled to engage in value destruction to preserve the channels of value creation. The paradox is such that destruction may be the path for preservation and creation, in that the effective neutralization of threats then helps assure that the structures and agents of value creation survive to continue their value-creating activities.

Armed forces in non-defense value creation

In the wider historical context, it should be noted that militaries have been responsible for the generation of phenomena that peacetime civilization takes for granted today, including economic markets and money-exchange (Graeber, 2012). In the 20th century, and indeed earlier in the industrial age (Alic et al., 2012), it became increasingly evident to politicians and to public managers alike that investments in the military were leading to substantial technological breakthroughs with benefits for civilian life (Mowery, 2010; Luchsinger & Bois, 2014). Even in the comparatively avant-garde domain of military spatial research, the spin-offs have been substantial, and Luchsinger and Blois enumerate several: global positioning satellite (GPS) navigation, mobile communications, fuels, weather observation, power sources, protective clothing, and visual-screen displays (2014). This stream of innovations, generating public value as they have, must be noted as a key contribution that armed forces make.

In fact, such spin-offs should be recognized as a form of positive externality, in that beneficiaries external to the immediate agents exist, who also reap some gains (Mowery, 2010; Hartley, 2012). Research has raised questions about the nature and genesis of such innovations. For example, do armed forces as public managerial institutions, including their scientists, technicians, and wider workforce (both uniformed and civilian) reach breakthroughs as part of a managed process or serendipity? (see Brown & Wilson, 1993). Similarly, is competition the driving force, as in the US-Soviet Space Race? Or rather is it that a constant and concerted effort in the absence of threat and competition a sufficient guarantor of momentum in innovation? (Alic et al., 1992). For example, a country with a comparatively rudimentary economy such as Pakistan has pursued technologically advanced projects such as a successful fighter aircraft program (JF-17) and also attained nuclear capabilities to deter international aggression (Kristensen et al., 2018; Chohan, 2019a).

In addition, the armed forces offer an important form of job creation in countries with large standing armies; so much so that the world's two largest employers are the US Department of Defense (DoD) with 3.2 million employees (measured by payrolls), and the Chinese People's Liberation Army (PLA) with 2.3 million employees, according to the World Economic Forum, which also lists the Indian Armed Forces as the world's ninth largest employer (Taylor, 2015). The employment aspect of the armed forces also serves a sociological function in creating upward mobility across class divisions (Caforio, 2018), notably in countries where social stratification is somewhat rigid (see Turkish example in Brown, 1989). In countries with mandatory conscription, such as Finland, South Korea, or Israel, citizens undergo an important socialization process and establish networks that may last their entire lives (Rosman, 2019; Caforio, 2018).

Furthermore, armed forces make heavy investments in the human resource development of their institutions, which can often have positive externalities as officials move out of the military hierarchy and into the civilian workforce (Rosman, 2019). For example, the University of New South Wales (UNSW) Canberra partners with the Australian Defense Force Academy (ADFA) to offer every Australian cadet the equivalent of a comprehensive undergraduate education (see Chohan, 2018). An investment in human resources results in even greater dividends when there is a general disparity between the quality of the armed forces' training and civilian private and public sector provision of HR training. An example of this is the Pakistan Air Force, which through extensive grooming, skills training, socialization, educational initiatives, and regularized programs, has groomed a workforce that has not just accomplished organizational goals (such as the indigenization of fighter aircraft, e.g.

JF-17), but also contributed to numerous civilian projects of national importance (see Chohan, 2019a, pp. 3–4).

Beyond this, the armed forces have a role in bolstering civil administration during periods of stress or heightened peacetime mobilization, including in disaster relief management (see Heaslip & Barber, 2014; Tatham & Rietjens, 2016). This often allows militaries to engage directly with the public in assisting both political and public managerial institutions to rescue, protect, or provide relief to the public. When executed well, this often reinforces the legitimacy and recognition of public value of armed forces, which are two nodes of the PV strategic triangle (Moore, 1995; see also the next section). Examples of this were witnessed during relief efforts of the US Army after the 2005 Hurricane Katrina (see Bowman et al., 2005), or in the Pakistan Army's efforts after the 2005 Kashmir Earthquake (Bowers, 2010). Disaster relief itself offers a very important lens for the study of public value, and it has already received extensive treatment in the broader public administration literature (see review in Simo & Bies, 2007); yet the armed forces contribution to this inquiry remains an underexplored issue (see an exception in Tanaka, 2013).

This allows for the advancement of a fourth proposition:

> *Proposition 4: Armed Forces can create value outside the realm of defense. These include innovations and spin-offs, employment, civil administrative support in crises, and even market-oriented activity*

A slightly more complex issue arises in the case of peacetime non-disaster public value, which includes the armed forces extending their mandates toward services that are usually provided by public managers or private entities (i.e. by the civilian state or the private market) in peacetime conditions. This might include sectors such as real estate, construction, consumer staples, and banking. Interesting examples of this can be found in the Pakistani context, where the Defense Housing Authority (DHA) zones in many cities are considered among the most well-managed residential areas, while *Fauji* or *Askari*[2] brand conglomerates engage in sectors as diverse as fertilizers, cereals, construction, banking, and insurance. Pakistani bureaucrats and politicians have raised concerns about this encroachment into civilian public managerial roles, but empirical studies have found that the capitalization of these conglomerates is quite small and of such a nature that they do not significantly impinge on (i.e. crowd out) civilian private or public investment (Hussain, 2017). For example, an octogenarian economic adviser to Prime Minister of Pakistan, Ishrat Hussain, has conducted econometric analyses on the share of economic activity and capitalization of Army conglomerates, and found that their share is miniscule at less than 4% of the overall capitalization (Hussain, 2017). This would suggest that political efforts to exaggerate the role of the army in non-defense goods and services provision has been at play, and that their size is overemphasized for political expediency (see Siddiqa, 2017). Nevertheless, it remains a constant issue of political interest in Pakistan that armed forces entities participate in market-based activity as well as public value creation usually found in the ambit of civilian administration in other countries.

The strategic triangle

With the foregoing dimensions of defense and non-defense public value creation of the armed forces having been given some consideration, it is particularly useful to situate the public managerial role of armed forces within the framework of Moore's strategic triangle (1994, 1995), with its importance as the "central symbol" of public value (Alford & O'Flynn, 2009, p. 173). The strategic triangle is premised on three nodes: a recognition of public value, a conferral of legitimacy, and operational resources. These are contextualized to armed forces public managers in Table 3.2.

Table 3.2 Strategic triangle for the armed forces

Number	Application	Example
Legitimacy	Armed forces must be perceived as guardians of the public's security and defense, acting as legitimate, disciplined, and vigilant institutions.	Armed forces work with other public manager institutions and stakeholders in society to maintain an acceptable level of security. They foster a culture of discipline and vigilance in their officer and soldier cadres.
Recognition of value	Armed forces gain recognition of the value that they can provide in the defense and non-defense domains.	Civilian administration, political structures, and civil society confer a recognition of the value provided by armed forces, but different groups and individuals ascribe different levels of value to defense as a public good.
Operation resources	Armed forces require a host of operating capabilities & resources, including budgetary, technical, weaponry, training, technological, physical, logistical, and material resources.	The operational resources of militaries support their discipline, vision, and morale. Material provisions, budgetary constraints, the risk of loss of life, training requirements, and physical/logistical requirements together make economic management of the armed forces a complex enterprise. In addition, armed forces gain or maintain an advantage by remaining at the edge of the technological curve.

Source: Author's research.

Armed forces 51

Legitimacy and recognition

One of the classic interpretations of the state's power is its monopoly on the legitimate use of violence (Williams, 1981), and part of the exercise of this monopoly materializes through the armed forces. With that in mind, militaries nevertheless enjoy differing levels of legitimacy in different publics. In some countries, the army is considered among the most trusted or legitimate public institutions. For example, in the United States, polling data suggests that people generally have a very favorable view of the military. According to Gallup, trust in the military has remained high with 73% expressing a "great deal" or "quite a lot" of trust and only 8% expressing "very little" trust (Gallup, 2019). By contrast, for the Supreme Court only 38% of respondents express a "great deal" or "quite a lot" of trust, while a full 20% express "very little trust" (Gallup, 2019). Similarly, research has found that 83% of respondents would say that they have confidence in the military "to act in the best interests of the public," tying them with scientists for the highest confidence of any group or institution (Rainie et al., 2019). This number has stayed fairly constant over the past 15 years, generally hovering in the 70%–80% range, which is an impressive feat for any public institution (Gallup, 2019). In another case, the Pakistani military is considered as the most trusted public institution and has the highest approval rating of any public office at 75%, while the judiciary (Supreme and High Courts of Pakistan) is the second-most trusted with an approval rating of 63%, according to a survey by the Pakistan Institute of Legislative Development and Training (PILDAT, 2015).

Public opinion may periodically swing in favor of or against the military due to sudden events. Malešič and Garb identify some general factors, including participation in wars, peacekeeping operations and missions, and crisis (disaster) management operations, structural reforms, and budget cuts, along with national idiosyncrasies (2018). After the 2005 Hurricane Katrina or the 2005 Kashmir Earthquake, the militaries of the United States and Pakistan received a broad message of support and solidarity for the execution of their humanitarian responsibilities to the public (Bowman et al., 2005; Bowers, 2010). Countries that contribute to successful peacekeeping forces also bolster their public managerial legitimacy both toward their own public and in publics abroad (Thakur, 2016). For example, Pakistan has joined more than 70 UN Peacekeeping Missions on five continents since 1947 (Peters, 2019), which has helped to support UN-backed efforts to ensure peace during periods of inter- and intra-state violence in high-conflict zones. This has helped to strengthen the international and domestic value creation efforts of the Pakistan Army through reinforcement of legitimacy (Peters, 2019).

Specifically with regard to the *recognition* of public value, it should be recalled that there are differences among citizens in terms of the value that will ascribe to public goods such as defense. Some citizens will ascribe a premium to security, while others will discount it, and so the "appropriate" level of defense provision will remain indeterminate to some degree but will nonetheless require a consideration of its provision (Bergstrom & Goodman, 1973; Hummel, 1990; Hartley, 2012). Yet militaries are always ultimately compelled to engage in value co-creation, as PVT terms it (see Moore & Khagram, 2004), which is to say, in partnership with other stakeholders. In fact, given the importance of earning legitimacy and recognition in the eyes of the public, it is only through co-creation and the mustering of "a coalition of sufficient support" (Benington & Turbitt, 2007, p. 383) that armed forces become effective public managers.

At times, however, a turbulent relationship can erupt between the civilian and military structures of government. In instances of a trust deficit between civil society and the military, Malešič and Garb make the assertion that it is militaries that are "marginalized" from civil society (2018, p. 144), and they attribute this to various factors, including all-volunteer military recruitment, criticism of the military in the media, the communication gap between the military and civil society, as well as instances of military corruption and scandals (Malešič & Garb, 2018). Militaries may also face dents in their legitimacy in instances where martial law is imposed (Gautam, 2018; Rukavishnikov & Pugh, 2018). Often times this is the product of disruptions in civil administration, political impasses, or of a break in the civilian-led processes of value creation, but it need not always be so, since *de facto* martial law can exist with civilian administrations in peculiar cases (see India's example in Gautam, 2018). In such instances, civil society responses are important from a PVT perspective because they represent one of the main agents of public value (Benington, 2009), and civil disobedience to military rule has been one of the most prominent elements in the disruption of martial law, in both colonial and post-colonial societies (Ryan, 2018). This is discussed in greater detail in a later section on armed forces as arbiters of value.

Operational resources

Armed forces require a host of operating capabilities and resources, including budgetary, technical, weaponry, training, technological, physical, logistical, and material resources. Contemporary defense forces are capital-intensive by nature, and this is all the more true for technology-intensive branches of the armed forces, such as air forces, which require the application of costly aviation instruments to defend and attack (Chohan, 2019a). Material provisions, budgetary constraints, the risk of loss of life, training requirements, and physical/logistical requirements together make economic management of the armed forces a complex enterprise. In addition, there is a constant pressure to upgrade existing technologies to remain at the cutting edge of innovation. As mentioned earlier, this is part of the reason that so much military advancement has found spin-offs and positive externalities in civilian life (Mowery, 2010; Luchsinger & Bois, 2014). Yet the ability of the public's fiscal resources to maintain such high-cost and constantly modernizing forces is invariably difficult. For example, the costs of aircraft continue to swell around the world, and predictions are that given the current cost inflation trajectory for major aircraft, only a handful of international air forces (with manned aircraft) shall remain within two decades. To this point, Norman Augustine famously remarked that with continued rising unit costs, by the year 2054, the entire US defense budget would purchase just one aircraft (see Hartley, 2012).

Solomon et al. describe the economic paradigm as follows: "the production of defence capabilities is based on the principles of constrained maximization," by which it is meant that there is "a process that maximizes the military capability achievable from a given budget with a given defence technology and a given set of input prices" (2008, p. 3). Operational resources of defense forces during deployment are themselves confronted by an amorphous aspect that necessitates oversight from both politicians and public managers. As an example, after the invasion of Iraq, the US force's military expenditures were managed in ways that raised concerns at the Office of the Special Inspector-General for Iraqi Reconstruction (SIGIR), finding several billions of funds missing or misused through a rigorous set of audits (see detailed work in Savage, 2013; Chohan, 2016).

That said, operational resources have not always been the exclusive determinant of war fighting, although they undoubtedly play important role (Hartley, 2010). PVT urges public managers to go beyond "narrow monetary outcomes to include that which benefits and is valued by the citizenry more generally" (Williams & Shearer, 2011, p. 1367; see also Moore & Khagram, 2004). Instead, operational resources of militaries support their discipline, vision, and morale. This is where PV's notions of a "value-seeking imagination" come amply to the fore (Moore, 1995, p. 22). Through an imaginative approach to the optimization of a constrained endowment of resources, public managers in the armed forces may successfully engage in the value-seeking exercise. Leadership, another important element in the public managerial drive (Benington & Turbitt, 2007; Wallis & Gregory, 2009), plays a seminal role in the success of armed forces in both peacetime and wartime (Horsfall, 1974).

From this, we may arrive at an insight provided by the strategic triangle: all three nodes are necessary for the armed forces to act as purposeful public managers, and none alone is sufficient for the fullest provision of public value by defense forces. Operational resources may be extremely important, but they are not the only determinant; rather, they bolster the ability of public managers to serve the public, foster a recognition for their work, and establish and maintain their legitimacy in the eyes of the public.

Armed forces as arbiters of value

There is a particular element to the power of armed forces as public managers, which pertains to their application of legitimate violence (Williams, 1981;

von Bredow, 2018), in that they have the potency to extract power from politicians through instruments of physical force. Because they are in a position to do so, they have the latent capability to both shape and challenge the established norms or rules of power in a society (Rukavishnikov & Pugh, 2018; von Bredow, 2018). This lends a tense air in some societies to civil-military relations (Malešič & Garb, 2018; von Bredow, 2018), which in the lexicon of the public administration is captured by the *politics-administration dichotomy* (Roberts, 1995; Chohan, 2017). The phenomenon of military coups has been known as far back as 876 BC, when the Biblical king Elah was murdered by the commander Zimri, only to take his own life so as to avoid an attack by his next-in-command Omri (Middleton, 2018). The coup d'état was immortalized in Western history in the Roman Ides of March, but has been repeated time and again since (Horsfall, 1974). As of the early 21st century, that incessant process of coups and counter-coups has meant that several coups are attempted around the world each year, often disrupting governments if not toppling them altogether.

PV's view on the primacy of political order is that democratically elected politicians must constitute the "final arbiters" of value (Moore, 1995, p. 38). Yet through coups and martial law, the armed forces constitute a type of non-traditional manager (NTM) that can wrest power away from politicians, dissolve assemblies, and impose martial law. Often this may have the premise (or pretext) of maintaining order or presenting resistance to an inside threat, and there is often a promise of restoration of civilian rule once "things calm down" (see Gautam, 2018; Rukavishnikov & Pugh, 2018; Ryan, 2018). Such military rule can involve a clampdown on the rights of the public (see Indian curfew example in Gautam, 2018). This speaks to the problem of "public value as rhetoric" (Chohan & Jacobs, 2018) where it has been argued that public managers might be prone to using PV as a legitimating device to wield greater power at the expense of democratic politicians (see Alford & O'Flynn, 2009). Aside from usurpation of democratic mandates from politicians, a martial law situation also weighs down on civil society, which is recognized as the third tenet of PVT, since the imposition of *de jure* or *de facto* martial law might curtail the rights of civilians, and might then constitute public value destruction.

This offers the occasion for a new proposition on the armed forces as public managers:

> *Proposition 5: Armed forces can breach the politics-administration dichotomy and become the final arbiters of value, but they risk distancing themselves from the values of their citizens*

This public value destruction is different from that discussed at the beginning of this chapter, where it was reasoned that the destructive power of armed forces might be channeled toward the assurance of security or the elimination of threats, such that value can be created by society itself. In this instance, by contrast, the military becomes a vehicle for public value destruction within its own borders (see Indian example in Gautam, 2018). Civil society may then pose a resistance to the armed forces because of a broader will to mobilize and challenge their legitimacy as arbiters. Two examples of this from the South Asian context can be suggested: first, in the lawyer's movement by the judiciary to challenge military rule in Pakistan (see previous chapter on the judiciary); and second, in the resistance of Kashmiri civil society to the occupation of Kashmir by Indian military forces in a state of de facto martial law (Gautam, 2018). To cite South Asian examples is not to limit the international scope of such disruptions and shifting dynamics of power. After all, they are experienced throughout the world and have been ongoing throughout recorded history (Horsfall, 1974; Middleton, 2018).

Conclusion

Armed forces were not treated as full-fledged public managers in the original references that PVT's founder Mark Moore made to "the generals" (1994, p. 298), since he contrasted them with his concept of public manager as civil administration. This reflected both his background (American) and that of his audience (Australian) as he sought to expound his early theorizations of public value. Yet as Poocharoen remarks, "governments define the scope and size of their bureaucracy differently; some would include the military and judiciary, while others would not" (2013, p. 333). In contexts outside of the traditional PVT scope of Western, liberal democracies, armed forces can often occupy a very central position within the architecture of public administration. For the purposes of this chapter, the initial assertion was that interesting insights about traditional PVT public managers could be gleaned by examining militaries as non-traditional managers (NTMs). This was evidenced in explorations of public value creation through potential destruction, the notion of collective security, the recognition of defense as a public good, the search for legitimacy by armed forces, non-defense forms of value creation, the constant limitations in armed forces' operational resources, the politics-administration dichotomy and martial law, and the question of militaries as arbiters of value.

Each of these aspects of armed forces' public value shows why perhaps Moore shouldn't have implied a distinction between public managers and "the generals" (1994, p. 298), if he were looking at the scope of public administration in a global context, not just because civil-military relations differ across countries (Malešič & Garb, 2018), but also because militaries can be among the most respected and trusted institutions in public administration in the eyes of the public (see American example in Gallup, 2019; Pakistani example in PILDAT, 2015). Sudden events can change the public's perception of the value provided by armed forces, as in natural disaster relief (Bowers 2010; Bowman et al., 2005), or in the breakdown of civil administration; not to mention after the trauma of a conflict.

There is an aspect of defense and non-defense value creation to armed forces. At the core, their provision of security addresses an elemental human value of survival; and phrased as the absence of insecurity (Baldwin, 1997) or the mitigation of risks, there is an inherent value that publics attribute to this, the ambiguity of measurement between individuals for public goods notwithstanding. The non-defense element of their value creation includes the research and development spin-offs that improve the quality of civilian life, the employment and human resource investments (including a socializing process, see Brown, 1989), and even in some cases the engagement with market-oriented activities or in lieu of civilian administration (Hussain, 2017).

Yet armed forces, as the name itself implies, are armed with both instruments as well as the potential for the legitimate use of "ordered violence" (Williams, 1981; von Bredow, 2018), which has long presented opportunities for the usurpation of power from democratically elected politicians, who in PVT have been deemed the "final arbiters of value" (Moore, 1995, p. 38). Because of this potential for taking the helm of administration, the armed forces can offer another look at the politics-administration dichotomy (Roberts, 1995) whereby they might impose martial law and alter the form of government. This can have repercussions on civil society, and so the responses provided by civil society take on a heightened importance, whether through the acceptance of a martial law arrangement or through public agitation against such a system. Williams and Shearer note that PVT's original motive was "an affirmation of managerial ingenuity and expertise, albeit within a binding democratic order and a finite resource base" (2011, p. 1372), but the civil-military relationship can be reshaped to challenge binding democratic orders in instances where the military takes the reins of power.

PVT has to confront such divergent arrangements around the world as part of its expansion into new contexts where public administration operates under different premises and through different logics (Chohan, 2019b), which is why Moore's initial assumptions about the shape of public administration face challenges in transposition to societies where armed forces develop alternate relationships with civil society, politicians, and other public managers. It may be observed, nevertheless, that many publics around the world hold their armed forces in high esteem (PILDAT, 2015; Gallup, 2019) and express a recognition of the value that these institutions provide, thereby conferring legitimacy to their position and acknowledging the need for operational resources to be provided for the creation of public value. Those operational resources are forever too scarce, even for the most generously endowed militaries, not least because the technological curve continues to advance, and the requirements of a modern force become costlier. In the same vein that dynamism is required to keep a military force operationally ready, a sense of dynamism also characterizes the relationship that armed forces have with civilian institutions and the public itself. In the spirit of PVT that helps "imbue public sector managers with a greater appreciation of the constraints and responsibilities within which they work" (2011, p. 1367), armed forces can draw a clearer understanding of their purpose through engagement with PVT. Reciprocally, as this chapter has determined, PVT has much to gain by drawing armed forces into the prism of its analysis as well.

Notes

1 For the purposes of simplicity and focus on their public managerial role, the terms "armed forces," "defense forces," and "military" are used interchangeably in this chapter, although they do connote different meanings in specific national and social contexts. For example, in countries such as Pakistan, the military may refer simply to the main standing army of ground forces, which would be a part of the joint services (tri-services) of army, navy, and air force that collectively comprise the armed forces. However, certain countries such as Australia and Israel refer to their armed forces as Defense Forces, even when engaging in military campaigns outside their boundaries and not on a defensive posture.
2 In the Urdu language, Fauji connotes "soldier" and Askari connotes "warrior." Both terms are used as brands for the conglomerates with majority shareholding of the Pakistan Army.

References

Alford, J., & O'Flynn, J. (2009). Making Sense of Public Value: Concepts, Critiques and Emergent Meanings. *International Journal of Public Administration, 32*(3–4), 171–191.
Alic, J. A., Branscomb, L. M., Brooks, H., & Carter, A. B. (1992). *Beyond Spinoff: Military and Commercial Technologies in a Changing World.* Cambridge, MA: Harvard Business Press.
Anderton, C., & Carter, J. (2009). *Principles of Conflict Economics.* Cambridge: Cambridge University Press.
Baldwin, D. A. (1997). The Concept of Security. *Review of Economic Studies, 23*(1), 5–26.
Benington, J. (2009). Creating the Public in Order to Create Public Value? *International Journal of Public Administration, 32*(3–4), 232–249.
Benington, J., & Turbitt, I. (2007). Policing the Drumcree Demonstrations in Northern Ireland: Testing Leadership Theory in Practice. *Leadership, 3*(4), 371–395.
Bergstrom, T. C., & Goodman, R. P. (1973). Private Demands for Public Goods. *The American Economic Review, 63*(3), 280–296.
Bouzenita, A. I., & Boulanouar, A. W. (2016). Maslow's Hierarchy of Needs: An Islamic Ccritique. *Intellectual Discourse, 24*(1), 1–15.
Bowers, W. J. (2010). Pakistan Earthquake Relief Operations: Leveraging Humanitarian Missions for Strategic Success. *Prism, 2*(1), 131–144.
Bowman, S., Kapp, L., & Belasco, A. (2005). *Hurricane Katrina: DOD Disaster Response.* Washington, DC: Congressional Research Service.
Box, R. C. (2003). Contradiction, Utopia, and Public Administration. *Administrative Theory & Praxis, 25*(3), 243–260.
Box, R. C. (2015). *Critical Social Theory in Public Administration.* London: Routledge.
Brown, J. (1989). The Military and Society: The Turkish Case. *Middle Eastern Studies, 25*(3), 387–404.

Brown, M. A., & Wilson, C. R. (1993). R&D Spinoffs: Serendipity vs. a Managed Process. *The Journal of Technology Transfer, 18*(3–4), 5–15.

Caforio, G. (2018). Military Officer Education. In G. Caforio (Ed.), *Handbook of the Sociology of the Military* (pp. 273–300). New York: Springer.

Cavelty, M. D., & Balzacq, T. E. (2016). *Routledge Handbook of Security Studies*. London: Routledge.

Chohan, U. W. (2016). The Idea of Legislative Budgeting in Iraq. *International Journal of Contemporary Iraqi Studies, 10*(1–2), 89–103.

Chohan, U. W. (2017). Independent Budget Offices and the Politics-Administration Dichotomy. *International Journal of Public Administration, 41*(12), 1009–1017.

Chohan, U. W. (2018). *The Roles of Independent Legislative Fiscal Institutions: A Multidisciplinary Approach*. (Doctoral Thesis), University of New South Wales (UNSW), Canberra.

Chohan, U. W. (2019a). Defense Economics: Perspectives on Air Forces, Air Defense & Aerial Warfare. *Anthropology of Peace & Violence eJournal: Social Science Research Network (SSRN), 19*(1), 1–13.

Chohan, U. W. (2019b). The FATF in the Global Financial Architecture: Challenges and Implications. *Monetary Economics: International Financial Flows, Financial Crises, Regulation & Supervision eJournal: Social Science Research Network (SSRN), 19*(1), 1–34.

Chohan, U. W. (2019c). *Public Value and Budgeting: International Perspectives*. London: Routledge.

Chohan, U. W., & Jacobs, K. (2018). Public Value as Rhetoric: A Budgeting Approach. *International Journal of Public Administration, 41*(15), 1217–1227.

Engerer, H. (2011). Security as a Public, Private or Club Good: Some Fundamental Considerations. *Defence and Peace Economics, 22*(2), 135–151.

Gallup. (2019). *Confidence in Institutions*. Washington, DC: Gallup.

Gautam, K. (2018). Martial Law in India: The Deployment of Military under the Armed Forces Special Powers Act. *Southwestern Journal of International Law, 24*(1), 117–131.

Graeber, D. (2012). *Debt: The First 5000 Years*. London: Penguin.

Graeber, D. (2015). *The Utopia of Rules*. Brooklyn, NY: Melville House.

Hartley, K. (2010). The Case for Defence. *Defence and Peace Economics, 21*(5–6), 409–426.

Hartley, K. (2012). Conflict and Defence Output: An Economic Perspective. *Revue d'économie politique, 122*(2), 171–195.

Heaslip, G., & Barber, E. (2014). Using the Military in Disaster Relief: Systemising Challenges and Opportunities. *Journal of Humanitarian Logistics and Supply Chain Management, 4*(1), 60–81.

Horsfall, N. (1974). The Ides of March: Some New Problems. *Greece & Rome, 21*(2), 191–199.

Hummel, J. R. (1990). National Goods versus Public Goods: Defense, Disarmament, and Free Riders. *The Review of Austrian Economics, 4*(1), 88–122.

Hussain, I. (2017). *Governing the Ungovernable: Institutional Reforms for Democratic Governance*. Oxford: Oxford University Press.

Hussein, K., Gnisci D., & Wanjiru J. (2004). *Security & Human Security: An Overview of Concepts and Initiatives*. Paris: OECD.

Jabeen, M., & Mazhar, M. S. (2011). Security Game: SEATO and CENTO as Instrument of Economic and Military Assistance to Encircle Pakistan. *Pakistan Economic and Social Review, 49*(1), 109–132.

Jakobsen, J. (2018). Is European NATO Really Free-Riding? Patterns of Material and Non-material Burden-Sharing after the Cold War. *European Security, 27*(4), 490–514.

Jones-Lee, M. (1990). Defence Expenditure and the Economics of Safety. *Defence Economics, 1*(1), 13–16.

Khan, M. A. (1964). The Pakistan-American Alliance: Stresses and Strains. *Foreign Affairs, 42*(2), 195.

Kristensen, H. M., Norris, R. S., & Diamond, J. (2018). Pakistani Nuclear Forces, 2018. *Bulletin of the Atomic Scientists, 74*(5), 348–358.

Kupchan, C. A. (1995). The Promise of Collective Security. *International Security, 20*, 52–61.

Luchsinger, V. P., & Blois, J. V. (2014). Spin-offs from Military Technology: Past and Future. *International Journal of Technology Management, 4*(1), 21–29.

Malešič, M., & Garb, M. (2018). Public Trust in the Military from Global, Regional and National Perspectives. In G. Caforio (Ed.), *Handbook of the Sociology of the Military* (Vol. 1, pp. 144–159). New York: Springer.

Marcuse, H. (1964). *One-dimensional Man: Studies in the Ideology of Advanced Industrial Society*. Boston, MA: Beacon Press.

Middleton, P. (2018). The "Noble Death" of Judas Iscariot: A Reconsideration of Suicide in the Bible and Early Christianity. *Journal of Religion and Violence, 6*(2), 245–266.

Moore, M. (1994). Public Value as the Focus of Strategy. *Australian Journal of Public Administration, 53*(3), 296–303.

Moore, M. (1995). *Creating Public Value: Strategic Management in Government*. Cambridge, MA: Harvard University Press.

Moore, M. (2014). Public Value Accounting: Establishing the Philosophical Basis. *Public Administration Review, 74*, 465–477.

Moore, M., & Khagram, S. (2004). *On Creating Public Value: What Business Might Learn from Government about Strategic Management*. Cambridge: John F. Kennedy School of Government, Harvard University.

Moore, M. H., Estrich, S. R., McGillis, D., & Spelman, W. (1984). *Dangerous Offenders: The Elusive Target of Justice*. Cambridge, MA: Harvard University Press.

Mowery, D. C. (2010). Military R&D and Innovation. In B. H. Hall & N. Rosenberg (Eds.) *Handbook of the Economics of Innovation* (Vol. 2, pp. 1219–1256). North-Holland: Elsevier.

Murray, W., & Mansoor, P. R. (2012). *Hybrid Warfare: Fighting Complex Opponents from the Ancient World to the Present*. Cambridge: Cambridge University Press.

Pakistan Institute of Legislative Development and Transparency (PILDAT). (2015). *Assessment of Democracy: Pakistan*. Islamabad: PILDAT.

Peter, M. (2019). *Peacekeeping: Resilience of an Idea*. New York: Palgrave Macmillan.

Poòcharoen, O. (2013). Bureaucracy and the Policy Process. In E. F. Araral, S., M. Howlett, M. Ramesh, & X. Wu (Eds.), *Routledge Handbook of Public Policy* (349–264). London: Routledge.

Rainie, L., Keeter, S., & Perrin, A. (2019). *Trust and Distrust in America*. Washington, DC: Pew Research Centre.

Roberts, A. (1995). "Civic Discovery" as a Rhetorical Strategy. *Journal of Public Policy Analysis and Management, 14*(2), 291–307.

Rosman, E. (2019). An Undergraduate School for the Nation: The Effect of Military Service on Veterans' Social Perceptions. *Nations and Nationalism*.

Rukavishnikov, V. O., & Pugh, M. (2018). Civil-military Relations. In G. Caforio (Ed.), *Handbook of the Sociology of the Military* (pp. 123–143). New York: Springer.

Ryan, L. (2018). Martial Law in the British Empire. In B. H. Hall & N. Rosenberg (Eds.) *Violence, Colonialism and Empire in the Modern World* (pp. 93–109). London: Palgrave Macmillan.

Savage, J. (2013). *Reconstructing Iraq's Budgetary Institutions: Coalition State Building after Saddam*. Cambridge: Cambridge University Press.

Siddiqa, A. (2017). *Military Inc.: Inside Pakistan's Military Economy*. Delhi: Penguin Random House India.

Simo, G., & Bies, A. L. (2007). The Role of Nonprofits in Disaster Response: An Expanded Model of Cross-sector Collaboration. *Public Administration Review, 67*(2), 125–142.

Solomon, B., Choinard, P., & Kerzner, L. (2008). *The Department of National Defense Strategic Cost Model: Vol ll – Theory and Empirics*. Ottawa: Centre for Operational Research & Analysis.

Tanaka, T. (2013). NHK's Disaster Coverage and Public Value from Below: Analyzing the TV Coverage of the Great East Japan Disaster. *Keio Communication Review, 35*(1), 23–37.

Tatham, P., & Rietjens, S. (2016). Integrated Disaster Relief Logistics: A Stepping Stone Towards Viable Civil–military Networks? *Disasters, 40*(1), 7–25.

Taylor, H. (2015). Who Is the World's Biggest Employer? The Answer Might Not be What You Expect. *World Economic Forum*, June 17.

Thakur, R. (2016). *The United Nations, Peace and Security: From Collective Security to the Responsibility to Protect*. Cambridge: Cambridge University Press.

van der Waal, Z., & van Hout, E. T. (2009). Is Public Value Pluralism Paramount? The Intrinsic Multiplicity and Hybridity of Public Values. *International Journal of Public Administration Review, 32*(3–4), 220–231.

von Bredow, W. (2018). The Order of Violence. Norms and Rules of Organized Violence and the Civil-Military Paradox. In G. Caforio (Ed.), *Handbook of the Sociology of the Military* (pp. 87–100). New York: Springer.

Wallis, J., & Gregory, R. (2009). Leadership, Accountability and Public Value: Resolving a Problem in "New Governance"?. *International Journal of Public Administration, 32*(3–4), 250–273.

Williams, R. M. (1981). Legitimate and Illegitimate Uses of Violence. In W. Gaylin, R. Macklin, & T. Powledge (Eds.) *Violence and the Politics of Research* (pp. 23–45). Springer.

Williams, I., & Shearer, H. (2011). Appraising Public Value: Past, Present and Futures. *Public Administration, 89*(4), 1367–1384.

Chapter 4

Multilateral public managers

Introduction

The aim of this chapter is to examine **public managers at multilateral institutions** as non-traditional managers (NTMs) attempting to create value for an international public. This chapter is thus a departure from domestic (national-level) public value creation, and looks instead at global and "wider notions of the public" (Chohan, 2019b, p. 40; see also Benington, 2009). The specific lens for examining multilateral NTMs is the International Monetary Fund (IMF, "the Fund"). However, the interconnectivity between the Fund and other organizations such as the World Bank (WB) (henceforth, collectively the "Bretton Woods Institutions," see also Widmaier, 2014) or the Financial Action Task Force (FATF) allows for a degree of similitude in the inquiry of these organizations as a class of global public managerial institutions (Woods, 2003; Peet, 2009; Widmaier, 2014; Chohan, 2019a). The chapter seeks to highlight how attempts to look at an aggregate international "public," which is in fact composed of many different national "publics," pose a peculiar set of challenges for PV scholars, since the underlying component publics may hold conflicting, contradictory, or even antagonistic values (see European Union example in Chohan, 2019b). As Moore himself noted, there is a need to examine "a public rather than the summation of individual aspirations" (Moore, 2014, p. 469), and this has been an area of heightened interest in the PV literature (Benington, 2009), because "putting it plainly, if we cannot identify the audience (the 'they') for whom value is being created, how can we be certain that we are effectively creating value for 'them'?" (Chohan, 2019b, p. 41).

Although the study of the IMF through a PVT lens has thus far remained wanting, it should be seen as part of a trend toward studying *supranational publics* where we find "a new set of challenges that are an order of magnitude greater because of the competing or divergent interests of the national 'publics' that are its constituents" (Chohan, 2019b, p. 40). *Supranational institutions* are an important lens in examining value-creation policies implemented "above" the nation-state, but the nascent public value research on the subject has cautioned that such institutions are fraught with challenges in delivering value for a multitude of national publics (Chohan, 2019, p. 40). By that account, going from EU-type supranational to the fully global system, a *weltgemeinschaft* or "world-public" in the fuller sense (Künneth & Beyerhaus, 1975), is yet a further order of magnitude more challenging than at the supranational level alone. The distinction being made is between "supranational" and "global," where the European Central Bank (ECB), European Union (EU), and Eurogroup (EG) are supranational entities responsible for a group of nations, while the IMF and World Bank are responsible for members states around the world (the IMF has more than 185 member states, see Fritz-Krockow & Ramlogan, 2007) and are thus as "global" as could be conceivable.

It is possible to raise some initial lines of questioning at this juncture. For one, if multilateral institutions represent PVT's public managers for a global public, then who are the "final arbiters" of value in a multilateral world? More fundamentally, what is the nature of this international "public" for which "value" is being created? The world can be messily divided into the Global North and Global South – a euphemistic allusion to the rich and poor countries – and it is messy because countries do move from the Global South to the North (South Korea or China, see Chohan, 2018a, 2018c), and from North to South as well (see Argentina in Blustein, 2006; Greece in Varoufakis, 2016). So can the dichotomized North and South truly be treated as a single "public?" As various authors have demonstrated, it is difficult enough to maintain supranational coherence within a body of 28 EU countries where each national public is so different, not least in terms of its endowments, its ambitions, its demographics, and of course its values (Varoufakis, 2016; Becker, 2017; Patomäki, 2017); what to make of the nearly 200 countries and the disparities both between and within them? Even confined to the domain of economics, and then also just in the specific ideology of neoliberalism, for example, are we to accept that the ethos of neoliberalism shall manifest similarly in Uganda (see analysis in Wiegratz, 2016) and New Zealand (see Wallis, 2010)? Equally contentiously, the chapter hints to the question of just whose values are being reflected in multilateral institutions, toward whom are these values being directed, and at the expense of whom. This alludes to questions of value destruction: do multilateral public managers become a conduit for the imposition of the values of one national public over another? Situating the multilateral public managers in PV terms thus holds significant promise for understanding one of the basic terms of "public value": the *public*.

PV's signature framework of the strategic triangle is pertinent in this regard because it helps to "structure thinking" about multilateral institutions (Alford & O'Flynn, 2009). How do public managers reconcile differences in values at a global level? How are operational resources diverted toward that end? What is the degree of legitimacy conferred on such institutions, and what is the level of recognition for their value-creation efforts? Finally, where are the structures of accountability for keeping a check on multilateral institutions? These are the sorts of difficult questions that must be posed regarding the role of multilateral public managers. The chapter thereby demonstrates how PV can become an important lens for addressing challenges that have arisen in the wake of globalization (see also Moore & Donahue, 2012; Chohan, 2019), not least in terms of the backlash that globalist (multilateral) institutions face today (Stiglitz & Pike, 2004; Margalit, 2012).

The task undertaken by this chapter is somewhat daunting in that it seeks to tease out various elements of value creation, articulation, rhetoric, leadership, destruction, legitimation, and survival. The IMF is, in this regard, an especially useful case for several reasons. First, the IMF is a distinct and important component within the modern international financial system and has had a long track record of nearly 75 years, having been established as part of the Bretton Woods system after 1945. Second, it is a "collective" composed of more than 185 countries, and deals with the monetary and fiscal concerns of each of them, to varying degrees (Fritz-Krockow & Ramlogan, 2007). Third, the experiences of dealing with the IMF, for better or worse, find similarity across many different countries that may otherwise not be lumped together with the same ease through other lenses (Woods, 2003; Ahamed, 2014; Moosa & Moosa, 2019c). Fourth, the IMF preserves a strong degree of connectivity with other international organizations such as the World Bank, International Financial Corporation, and newer politicized institutions such as the Financial Action Task Force (FATF) as well (Peet, 2009; Danaher, 2011; Chohan, 2019a). Fifth, given that there is much more to the work of the IMF than it would itself articulate (Peet, 2009), a PVT approach toward this multilateral institution is warranted since PV is a theory for exploring how people "think and feel about society" (Meynhardt, 2009, p. 193); and given that the IMF has had an impact on countless lives, particularly so in the developing world, PVT should do justice to its duty to discern how the lived experience of publics under IMF-imposed policies has led them to think and feel about society.

In view of the ambition of this chapter to situate the public manager of the world-public *weltgemeinschaft* (Kunneth & Beyerhaus, 1975) within PV frameworks, the structure has been laid out as follows. At first, certain descriptive elements of the IMF are presented as a public managerial institution, which shall allow PV scholarly approaches to tease out elements that will be explored in subsequent sections. Thereafter, the issue of the articulation of values by global citizens shall be considered in the theoretical terms provided by PVT. It is in this section that the propositional method will be followed, but somewhat differently in this chapter than in others: rather than offering novel propositions regarding multilaterals, it will draw upon the work of Chohan (2019b, pp. 40–50) to derive four propositions made regarding supranational entities, and then superimpose the IMF onto those PV propositions, to see the degree to which they are reflected (often to a much larger extent) at the global level via multilateral institutions. After this, certain problems of public value, including the challenge of leadership and the nature of PV rhetoric, shall be examined in light of their pertinence to multilateral NTMs. In all of this, an emphasis will be on developing countries because of (1) the disproportionate impact of IMF policies on the developing world (Blustein, 2003; Woods, 2014), and (2) the need for public value research to emphasize the experiences of developing countries as they may differ from those of developed ones (Samaratunge & Wijewardene, 2009).

Subsequently, the strategic triangle (Moore, 1995) shall be deployed to consider the nature of legitimacy for multilateral public managers, including a reciprocity between them and national-level politicians (Vreeland, 2003), along with broader questions about their recognition, and finally, about their operational resources and how they influence the capital and resource endowments of the publics with whom they deal. This sets the tone for the next section in which the IMF lens can shed light on three aspects of PVT: PV leadership (Wallis & Gregory, 2009), rhetoric in PV (Alford & O'Flynn, 2009), and PV destruction (Spano, 2009), with a consideration of how each of these impede the exercise of value creation for the world-public. Ultimately, this then raises questions in the concluding section about the survivability of multilateral institutions and of globalization in the longer-run (Stiglitz & Pike, 2004; Margalit, 2012), should they not address those problems of public value creation that constitute their concern.

The IMF as institution of multilateral public managers

By its own account, the IMF is "a cooperative of 185 member countries, whose objective is to promote world economic stability and growth," and it aims to provide its members with "macroeconomic policy advice, financing in times of balance of payments need, and technical assistance and training to improve national economic management" (Fritz-Krockow and Ramlogan, 2007, p. 1). The IMF portrays itself as a lender of last resort to struggling economies. Yet its role has evolved into much more (Lee, 2002; Danaher, 2011), and it has had an enormous impact on the world economy, which is to say, the value creation of the largest public. In delineating the importance of multilateral institutions such as the IMF, Woods stresses that "the procedures adopted by [the IMF and similar] institutions are central to the debate about global economic justice" (2003, p. 1), which means that their adherence to their stipulated goals and to the mechanisms by which they purportedly create value for the public must be given due attention. At the same time, the effects of its dealings have fallen disproportionately on the developing world (Woods, 2003, 2014; Barro & Lee, 2005), with both multifaceted and even value-destructive effects on the level of global inequality and development (Peet, 2009; Moosa & Moosa, 2019b, 2019c).

The study of the IMF's problems as they manifest in the developing world is not new (see Payer, 1975), but it gained increasing momentum after the 1990s when massive economic failures erupted across the developing world that were at least partly attributable to policies imposed by the IMF (Stone, 2003; Blustein, 2003, 2006; Vreeland, 2003; Woods, 2003). This momentum was redoubled after the 2008 financial crisis, when concerns were raised about global financial institutions as a whole (Peet 2009; Woods 2014; Moosa & Moosa, 2019b). As Lee surmises,

> given the IMF 's diminished currency, following its failure to predict or effectively manage a series of major financial crises in the latter half of the 1990s, authoritative leadership will be essential for the restoration of the IMF's credibility with member states and investors alike.
>
> (2002, p. 285)

Moosa and Moosa argue that, on the one hand, "if the IMF is judged by the declared objectives of eradicating poverty, boosting growth, enhancing social expenditure and raising the standard of living, then it has been a dismal failure," but on the other hand,

> if it is judged by the undeclared objectives of looting domestic assets, impoverishing developing countries, imposing neoliberal ideas on developing countries and having free access for the corporate "west" to sources of raw materials and markets, then it has been a spectacular success.
>
> (Moosa & Moosa, 2019c, p. 165).

But what is the basis of criticizing the IMF for international public value destruction? Lee categorizes the criticisms of the IMF under three headings: first, that it has overstretched its mandate of bringing monetary stability too far by instead exacerbating socioeconomic imbalances in societies; second, the conditions that the IMF has imposed have at times backfired spectacularly and failed to deliver economic growth; and third, the degree of transparency and accountability of the IMF itself is somewhat dubious and does not cohere with the supposed transparency it demands of nations themselves (Lee, 2002). Each of these shall be considered from a PVT perspective in later sections, but it should also be added that numerous empirical studies (see review in Barro & Lee, 2005) find that the IMF often stalls economic growth and has a somewhat negative effect on the rule of law and democracy (Vreeland, 2003; Barro & Lee, 2005).

Yet in identifying any initial criticisms of the IMF, it is also important to note what its defendants claim are its value-creating propositions. For example, Dresner observes that the overall conclusion to be drawn from the 2008 Financial Crisis is that the current system of economic governance has, despite many failings, worked out to the extent that "multilateral economic institutions performed well in crisis situations to reinforce open economic policies, especially in contrast to the 1930s" (2012, p. 4). Furthermore, "while there are areas where governance has either faltered or failed, on the whole, the system has [...] has worked better than expected because the distribution of power, institutions and ideas has changed less than is commonly understood" (Dresner, 2012, p. 4). Lee observes several generalizable justifications offered by the IMF and by its supporters; noting first that the IMF "could not ignore the need for internal structural reforms in the crisis-hit economies because these were the root causes of the crisis," and then adding that the IMF cannot "avoid the imposition of monetary tightening and austerity because of the need to offset the huge cost of financial restructuring" (2002, p. 287). From a PV perspective, this argument would suggest that the multilateral public managers are only stepping in when public managers and politicians at the national level are failing in their efforts to create value for the domestic publics.

In other words, the IMF's assertion is that a greater onus must be put on national-level public managers and politicians to fix their publics' problems, in which case the IMF's technocrats would not need to step in for assistance in the first place. Some critics of PVT raise a concern in claiming that public value's tacit predilection is to pretend "that there are no political tensions that cannot be resolved through sophisticated technocracy" (Oakley et al., 2006, p. 3), but in the case of the IMF's technocracy, as Lee highlights, "there have been repeated calls from the USA and beyond for the IMF and the World Bank to abandon crisis-lending and to retreat 'back to basics'" (2002, p. 290; see also Woods, 2003). What is important to emphasize is that the IMF sets *conditionalities* for lending to countries (Vreeland, 2003), and those conditions often have a significant impact on societies, distorting or reforming (depending on the point of view) the borrowing countries in structural ways, because of the IMF's ambition to address the causes rather than the mere symptoms of economic malaise. This line of reasoning has come under intense criticism (Lee, 2002; Blustein, 2003, 2006; Vreeland, 2003; Woods, 2003, 2014; Barro & Lee, 2005; Rapkin & Strand, 2006; Peet, 2009; Danaher, 2011; Widmaier, 2014), and shall be discussed in later sections.

So how have public managers (as people) at the IMF treated their constraints and responsibilities? It should be recalled that public value has sought above all to humanize and empower public managers, "to help imbue public sector managers with a greater appreciation of the constraints and responsibilities within which they work" (Williams & Shearer, 2011, p. 1367). There are several important works which seek to highlight the public managerial ethos of people working at the IMF, including their ostensibly good intentions to help poor countries, their talk of assisting the distressed and impoverished, and so forth (Blustien, 2003, 2006; Ahamed, 2014). A recurring observation in this literature is that public managers at the IMF think of their institution as generally doing its best given a complex world with many moving parts, and they appreciate the mission of the IMF in helping to create a more stable international financial system that assists crisis-hit economies to combat global poverty (Blustein, 2003, 2006; Ahamed, 2014). However, as anthropological examinations of bureaucracy (see review in Graeber 2015) have found, the individual aspirations of selfless bureaucrats need not automatically culminate in selfless or caring bureaucracies (Graeber, 2015). The problem is in fact more acute at the IMF, as Momani observes, because of the conspicuous absence of IMF staff – the human public managers behind the multilateral institution – in its plans or proposals for reform (Momani, 2007). This, in turn, raises a query about who it is at the IMF that is creating value, and for whom is it that they create value?

Who creates value for whom?

PVT urges managers to respond to the values that are articulated by citizens so that there is "a shift from a culture that accepts public acquiescence in decision making to one that expects active citizen endorsement" (Stoker, 2006, p. 47). This is in part why it has been described as "a comprehensive approach to thinking about public management and about continuous improvement in public services" (Constable et al., 2008, p. 9). In Moore's words, PV should be seen "a framework that helps us connect what we believe is valuable and requires public resources, with improved ways of understanding what our 'publics' value and how we connect to them" (Moore, 1995, p. 4). It also urges them to go beyond "narrow monetary outcomes to include that which benefits and is valued by the citizenry more generally" (Williams and Shearer, 2011, p. 1367; see also Moore & Khagram, 2004). In that spirit, this section alludes to the questions of just whose values are being reflected in multilateral institutions, toward whom are these values being directed, and at the expense of whom.

In a similar vein to Chohan's study of supranational entities (2019b, pp. 40–61), multilateral bodies face difficulties in addressing values given the plurality of the publics that their mandates subsume. Chohan offers a set of propositions about supranational managers that warrant mention at this juncture, and they shall be compared systematically with the case of the IMF for the multilateral context (as opposed to supranational; see Chohan, 2019b, pp. 40–61). Two will be discussed immediately in this section, while two shall receive treatment through Moore's strategic triangle in the following section (see strategic triangle in Moore, 1995; Alford & O'Flynn, 2009). The propositions derived from Chohan's supranational study (2019b, pp. 40–61) are also enumerated in Table 4.1.

The first proposition is that "supranational public managers are not just unbeholden to politicians of any electorate; they may also have goals that directly contradict or oppose those of national-level politicians and public managers" (2019b, p. 46). This is equally true for the IMF, because the Fund may

Table 4.1 Derived propositions for multilateral institutions

THEME	SUPRANATIONAL PROPOSITION	MULTILATERAL (IMF) APPLICATION
ACCOUNTABILITY	"Supranational public managers are not just unbeholden to politicians of any electorate; they may also have goals that directly contradict or oppose those of national-level politicians and public managers" (Chohan, 2019b, p. 46)	Equally true for the IMF, because the Fund may prioritize factors different from those valued by the public, such as exchange rate (devaluation), austerity programs, opening of local markets to trade, and cutbacks on social expenditure, which may go against the values articulated by the publics to national-level politicians.
IMBALANCES BETWEEN PUBLICS	"Imbalances between member states accentuate the conflicts about public value creation" (Chohan, 2019b, p. 48).	Even more true at the global (multilateral) level, since the imbalances between countries are starker worldwide than they are in any supranational regional block (such as the EU). These divergences are accentuated due to the absence of a global surplus recycling mechanism (SRM) that would mitigate inequalities by recycling wealth flows. Therefore, the ability of the IMF and other multilaterals to address the values of the world's constituent publics is even more restrained due to a wider scope. Because of this, there is a risk of public value destruction as the IMF engages with countries in a manner and with a mindset that is more appropriate for certain countries than for others.
OPERATION RESOURCES	"National politicians and public managers surrender public value-creating operational capabilities to supranational public managers, which weakens them even as they are still held to account by citizens" (Chohan, 2019b, p. 50).	The surrender of operational resources to multilateral institutions can be stark when a country is in economic distress and requires external assistance. Countries that enter into IMF programs are forced to adhere to constraints and make "structural adjustments," which constrains the operational resources available to national-level politicians and public managers for value creation. Their hands may be tied even on basic provisions of value to the public. Yet the public's displeasure is often diverted toward national-level politicians, who must bear the public's outrage even though they do not have the same control over their economic machinery once under the auspices of an IMF program.

THEME	SUPRANATIONAL PROPOSITION	MULTILATERAL (IMF) APPLICATION
LOSS OF TRUST IN PUBLIC MANAGERS	"Supranational public managers face a difficulty of legitimization in the eyes of citizens, and this loss of trust is seized upon by politicians to varying degrees" (Chohan, 2019b, p. 51).	The IMF also faces a difficulty of legitimization in the eyes of citizens in counties that are undertaking IMF programs; but whereas some national-level politicians may seize upon that loss of trust, other politicians in fact use the IMF as cover for implementing politically difficult programs. Yet the IMF itself draws the ire of many publics when it imposes austerity and other difficult policies on them, leading ultimately to heightened distrust of the IMF itself.

Source: Author's research; Derivation from Chohan (2019b, pp. 40–61).

prioritize factors different from those valued by the public, such as exchange rate devaluation, austerity programs, opening of local markets to trade, and cutbacks on social expenditure (Lee, 2002; Blustein, 2006; Moosa & Moosa, 2019b). A telling IMF-oriented example might lie in *social protection*, which refers to policies that serve the public with a safety net in times of hardship. The degree to which social protection is offered differs greatly between countries and is generally a function of their level of economic development. Public value scholars remark that there is a need to "rebuild public confidence in political institutions, and the most powerful way to do that is to seek active citizen endorsement of the policies and practices of public bodies" (Stoker, 2006, p. 48). But as Moosa and Moosa observe, "the IMF has been criticized for promoting policies that weaken social protection," and it is criticized "by academics, civil society organizations and international organizations," for the "adverse effect on public spending on health and education," that the IMF's conditionalities and policies entail (Moosa & Moosa, 2019b, p. 111; see also Vreeland, 2003).

As a former economist at the Financial Institutions Division of the Bureau of Statistics at the IMF, Moosa's analysis demonstrates that the Fund's policies, "including spending cuts and redirection, have an adverse effect on the ability of people to pay for private healthcare through austerity, poverty and the rising cost of healthcare" (see Moosa & Moosa, 2019b, p. 112). In aggregate economic terms, IMF operations reduce the per capita amount of consumption on healthcare (Lee, 2002; Vreeland, 2003; Barro and Lee, 2005; Moosa & Moosa, 2019b). Politicians at the local level may find austerity measures unpalatable, given the reprisals of citizens to the harshness of such measures and the value they erode. In such cases, politicians are reflecting the values of citizens, but the multilateral public managers might trample over the aspirations and needs of the public. In essence, a conflict may lie between what is valued by citizens, and what the IMF imposes as policy conditionality.

The second supranational proposition is that "imbalances between member states accentuate conflicts about public value creation" (Chohan, 2019b, p. 48). This refers to the problems of diversity among the constituent members of a supranational entity, whose publics may diverge in substantial ways, including in size, level of development, culture, and of course public values. This is no less true for multilateral public manager institutions such as the IMF, where country diversity makes it difficult for them to address the values articulated by each public, since there may be conflicting or even contradictory values held not just within publics but also between them. Is a rich country to articulate identical values to a poor one? A large one to a small one? Evidently, the summation of publics poses a challenge to PV creation efforts since the constituent publics prioritize different things at different times. For example, national-level public managers may be hesitant to open local markets to international competition because it would decimate local industry and result in a significant loss of jobs. Yet IMF pressure may force the hand of these national-level managers because of the IMF goal of internationalizing global trade (Fritz-Krockow & Ramlogan, 2007), which adheres to the values of larger economies rather than smaller ones. In another example, the IMF may force a country to devalue its currency and fall in line with "market-determined rates" (Lee, 2002; Fritz-Krockow & Ramlogan, 2007), which may collapse a public's purchasing power. While this may be acceptable in certain situations, smaller developing countries already reeling from high inflation may be loath to voluntarily devalue their currency while facing macroeconomic crisis (although see Argentinian counter-example in Blustein, 2003, 2006).

On this account, Chohan also observes that "citizens feel the pinch of this inequality in deficit nations in a variety of ways, but most notably in the services that public managers provide, such as wages, pensions, education, transport, healthcare, and various other public goods" (2019, p. 49). This puts an undue pressure on civil society in already crisis-afflicted or impoverished societies, and fails to reflect their values and aspirations for development. Chohan's second proposition (2019, p. 48) on supranational entities makes due reference to the concept of *surplus recycling mechanisms* (SRMs) as posited by Varoufakis (2016; see also Chohan, 2018c). Evidently, the world does not have an integrated SRM to flow money in a manner that addresses egregious international disparities (Danaher, 2011; Chohan 2018c), and to even suggest such a concept for "economic justice" in the world is likely to be met with derision in some quarters (see Woods, 2003, p. 1). In fact, it has long been argued (see Payer, 1975) that the IMF perpetuates what are known as *debt traps*, which is quite the opposite of an SRM in that debt traps extract further resources from deficit countries and redistribute them to the existing wealthy surplus countries (Varoufakis, 2016; Chohan, 2018c). Taking a step back, insofar as public value requires a multidirectional and active exchange of perspectives (van der Waal and van Hout, 2009; Beck Jorgensen & Vrangbaek

2011), there are far greater complications at the global level due to both the multiplicity of national perspectives (even when categorized into blocs, see Stone, 2003) as well as the asymmetries in the relative powers of nations. The substantive "negotiation process" that PV necessitates (Moore, 1994, 1995; Moore & Khagram, 2004; Talbot, 2009) is more urgently required but equally less feasible at this level.

The third proposition offered by Chohan regarding supranational entities pertains to operational resources, which are argued to be surrendered by national-level public managers to supranational ones, even though the blame for the failure of the ensuing policies rests with the politicians. Thus, the reprisals of citizens (whether physically or electorally) are targeted toward politicians, even though they do not have the operational resources to execute value creation as they might have once had (2019, p. 50). This is discussed in further detail the next section on the strategic triangle. The fourth proposition offered by Chohan pertains to the ultimate loss of trust in supranational public managers due to the "difficulty in legitimization" that they face after persistent failures to respond to the values articulated by citizens (2019, p. 51), and this too is discussed in the next section through the prism of the strategic triangle.

The strategic triangle

With respect to the foregoing dimensions of value-creation hindrances, it is particularly useful to situate the public managerial role of multilateral organizations within the framework of Moore's strategic triangle (1994, 1995), given its importance as the "central symbol" of public value (Alford & O'Flynn, 2009, p. 173). This is particularly true for contextualizing two of Chohan's supranational propositions as they might be transposed onto the multilateral context. The strategic triangle is premised on three nodes: a recognition of public value, a conferral of legitimacy, and operational resources. These are contextualized for multilateral public managers in Table 4.2.

Legitimacy: reciprocal legitimation

Trust and legitimacy are argued to be the eventual goal of public value (Talbot, 2009, p. 168), and critics of public value theory raise a concern in saying that public value's subjacent tendency may be to pretend "that there are no political tensions that cannot be resolved through sophisticated technocracy" (Oakley et al., 2006, p. 3), even when the technocratic legitimacy of the IMF contends with the national politics of countries where they impose programs. Meynhardt has observed that "legitimization by numbers may appear a less complex challenge than facing the challenge of a pro-active dialogue about 'why our work is valuable to society'" (2009, p. 214). The struggle for multilateral public managers therefore becomes one of articulating why their

Table 4.2 Strategic triangle for the multilateral institutions (IMF)

Number	Application
Legitimacy	Multilateral institutions face a difficulty of legitimization in the eyes of citizens whenever the policies they impose cause undue public value destruction. Yet some politicians seek reciprocal legitimation with the IMF, using its recommendations to mete out policies that would otherwise be politically unfeasible. Meanwhile, the IMF garners legitimation for its role by presenting politicians with adjustment programs that will supposedly fix the economic problems that the public faces. Over time, however, if citizens do not recognize meaningful value creation, there is a loss of trust in both national politicians and multilaterals.
Recognition of value	There may be a divergence between the recognition of multilaterals in the short- and long-run. For example, in times of crisis, there may be a recognition of the value that the IMF can provide to stabilize financial systems and bail out governments. In the long-run, austerity and other reductions in social expenditures, which are important to citizens, may lead to a refusal to recognize the value in IMF propositions. Yet there are some aspects of IMF value creation related to maintaining international economic stability that do deserve mention. At the same time, the transparency and accountability of the IMF itself is a notable gap that perpetuates declining recognition of its value proposition.
Operation resources	Countries that enter into IMF programs are forced to adhere to constraints and make "structural adjustments," which constrains the operational resources available to national-level politicians and public managers for value creation. Their hands may be tied even on basic provisions of value to the public. Politicians and national-level public managers may ultimately attempt to wrest back control of surrendered operational resources from multilateral institutions.

Source: Author's research.

work is valuable to a composite, global society. They must engage in what Lowndes et al. call the "renewal of citizen consent" (2006, p. 552); and what Benington and Turbitt term the "coalition of sufficient support" that must be forged to generate legitimacy in the eyes of the public (2007, p. 383). In fact, it should be noted that sometimes there is a dynamic of reciprocal legitimation between national-level public managers and politicians, on the one hand, and multilateral institutions, on the other. The IMF lends credibility to the politicians and public managers of countries in international eyes, and allows them to push through policies that might otherwise be unpalatable to the public (see Stone 2003; Vreeland, 2003). What Vreeland's empirical study has found corroborates the notion of reciprocal legitimation, thus:

> [IMF] programs hurt economic growth and redistribute income upward. By bringing in the IMF, governments gain political leverage – via conditionality – to push through unpopular policies. For certain constituencies, these policies dampen the effects of bad economic performance by redistributing income. But IMF programs doubly hurt others who are less well off: they lower growth and exacerbate income inequality.
>
> (Vreeland, 2003, p. 41)

The underlying dynamic of multilateral public manager legitimacy is thus bi-directional. On the one hand, the IMF wishes to foster a legitimacy for its policies through public managers and politicians of developing nations, particularly through at least short-term economic successes (see Argentina in the 1990s in Blustein, 2006). On the other hand, politicians and public managers of developing nations seek to legitimize difficult, value-destructive, or anti-public economic policies with the support of the IMF. This allows both of them to rationalize one another's legitimacy and even suggests an ostensible recognition for their value to the public. This is expressed diagrammatically in Figure 4.1.

PVT asserts that politicians are the "final arbiters" of value (Moore, 1995, p. 38), but in reciprocal legitimation, the politicians themselves are seeking legitimation from the multilateral public managers. Are the politicians in these instances the drivers of policies that may destroy value, or are the multilaterals using politicians to drive those policies through? This is a particularly

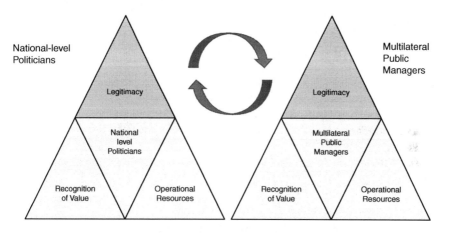

Figure 4.1 Reciprocal legitimation: multilaterals and national politicians.
Source: Author's research; see also Stone (2003), Vreeland (2003).

difficult question to tease out, and the literature seems to suggest that there is a different causal pathway in each country case study (Stone, 2003; Vreeland, 2003; Woods, 2003; Barro & Lee, 2005; Blustein, 2006; Danaher, 2011), with different local dynamics defining the interplay of legitimation between national politicians and supranational public managers (see also review in Chohan, 2019b, pp. 40–45). Ultimately, however, contrary to Moore's expectations of democratic political primacy in many developed nations (Moore, 1994), the nature of democratic maturity in developing nations is less definite and sustained (see critical discussions in Samaratunge & Wijewardena, 2009; Chohan, 2019b), which leaves politicians of developing countries more amenable (read: susceptible) to policies imposed by multilateral public managers. It is difficult, therefore, to state the extent to which multilateral public managers impinge on democracy, even though the arguments are strong that they do (Vreeland, 2003; Blustein, 2003, 2006; Danaher, 2011).

If politicians and the multilaterals sustain an equilibrium of reciprocal legitimation for some time, but the outcomes of their policies rebuke the values of society or destroy excessive public value, then ultimately both the multilaterals and national politicians risk losing legitimacy. Public value scholars remark that there is a need to "rebuild public confidence in political institutions, and the most powerful way to do that is to seek active citizen endorsement of the policies and practices of public bodies" (Stoker, 2006, p. 48). In addition to being the third pillar of public value theory (see Benington, 2009; Chohan, 2019, pp. 40–59), civil society might be a much more appropriate arbiter of public value than politicians when the democratic process is not representative of the aspirations of the people. This is indeed why "IMF riots" have occurred for at least the past 40 years (Blustein, 2003, 2006; Barro & Lee, 2005; Moosa & Moosa, 2019b), since civil society has found the aftershocks of IMF-induced policies to be unpalatable and sometimes blatantly destructive toward the public (Lee, 2002; Vreeland, 2003; Danaher, 2011).

Recognition of value: the urgent and the important

The recognition of value provided by the multilateral public managers is best bifurcated into short- and long-run periods; the urgent and the important, so to speak. For the urgent, there may be occasion for the public, national politicians, and national public managers, to recognize the need for an immediate bailout, even with strings attached (Woods, 2003, 2014; Rapkin & Strand, 2006). This would reflect the urgency of the need for a public manager intervention by multilaterals, and the recognition may be different among the national-level agents. Examinations of historical IMF interventions suggest that national-level public managers detect the need for bailouts more quickly (see also Blustein, 2003; Stone, 2003; Barro & Lee, 2005), but this is a function of the access to technocratic expertise and rigorous forecasts that they possess compared to politicians and citizens (see also Chohan, 2018b).

Politicians must then generate political will to accept an IMF package, and this has been particularly true in recent years as the track record of the IMF has fallen into increasing disrepute (Woods, 2014; Moosa & Moosa, 2019b).

However, taking a look at factors in the long-run, including the impact of austerity and other reductions in social expenditures (Vreeland, 2003), the public may be more reticent to recognize IMF value-contribution. For this reason, IMF riots may break out (Moosa & Moosa, 2019a, 2019b), and a restive population may articulate its rejection of IMF-imposed policies and demand the toppling of politicians themselves, whether through elections or through force. Incidences of "IMF riots" can be cited as far back as the 1980s, and they occur frequently even unto the present day, from countries as diverse as Argentina, Haiti, South Africa, Indonesia, Costa Rica, Chile, Pakistan, and Ukraine, to cite but a few (Ahamed, 2014; Moosa & Moosa, 2019c).

The nuance in the argument is that there is a time-inconsistent preference for the IMF's interventions, reflecting the desperation for bailout assistance in crisis situations. In the short-run, an emergency package may be required, but in the long-run the costs (economic, social, and political) may far outweigh the size of any loan. It has also been remarked that countries that follow IMF policies, and become the "darling" of multilateral economic institutions, later risk facing disastrous economic outcomes. The most vivid example of this was Argentina (see detailed chronology in Blustein, 2006), when the country's conformity with IMF recommendations led to a boom in the late 1990s but a spectacular collapse a few years later in 2001. The public's recognition of the IMF's value thus shifted from the favorable to the unfavorable over that period (Blustein, 2006). It must also be noted that the relationship between the IMF and Argentina persists to the present day (Moosa & Moosa, 2019b), and Argentina is also, as of this writing, beset with renewed economic hardship (Moosa & Moosa, 2019c).

To keep the balance of argument, a counter-assessment should be noted in the other value-creation aspects of the IMF and other Bretton Woods multilaterals, including keeping the overall economic system, unequal and unfair as it may be, in a kind of open and dynamic equilibrium. Partisans of the status quo in global economic governance (as identified by Dresner, 2012) argue that multilaterals have been quite successful in doing so, noting that "one of the primary purposes of multilateral economic institutions is to provide global *public goods* – including keeping barriers to cross-border exchange low" (Dresner, 2012, p. 4, emphasis added; see also discussion on public goods in the previous chapter on the armed forces), further arguing that "an open global economy lessens the stagnation that comes from a financial crisis, preventing a downturn from metastasizing into another Great Depression" (Dresner, 2012, p. 4).

Finally, the recognition of multilateral public value depends on transparency and accountability, which in PVT are shown to be important determinants of value creation (Douglas & Meijer, 2016). One of the three general criticisms of the IMF (according to Lee, 2002) is that the Fund itself does not adhere to levels of transparency and accountability that it chooses to set for developing countries during their programs. In other words, it does not itself prescribe to the level of accountability that it sets for others; and from a PV point of view, this bodes ill for the recognition of its PV since transparency is considered a precursor for effective value creation (Douglas & Meijer, 2016; Chohan, 2018b). If multilateral institutions are not forthcoming about the way that they proceed with their stipulated mandates, then politicians and public managers in countries that are undertaking IMF programs will be hard pressed to persuade the public that the IMF is engaged in value creation.

Operational resources: surrender and obsolescence

Chohan offered a proposition regarding supranational public managers that over time, national-level public managers and politicians would come to surrender more and more of their operational resources to supranational entities (Chohan, 2019, p. 50), even though the blame for the failure of the ensuing policies would be shared between supranational institutions and local politicians. Thus, the reprisals of citizens (whether physically or electorally) would also be targeted toward national politicians, even though these politicians would no longer have had the operational resources to execute value creation as they might have once had (2019, p. 50; see also Becker, 2017). This conundrum resonates with multilateral institutions, particularly in the case of developing countries that enter into "structural adjustment programmes" with the WB/IMF. These interventions require adherence to strict fiscal rules (see also Lee, 2002; Barro & Lee, 2005; Chohan, 2018b), and other forms of policy constraints. They might also involve the deployment of technocrat public managers from the multilateral institutions into the national economic machinery, thereby overriding national public manager leadership and capabilities (Stone, 2003), which speaks to the criticism of PVT that it might be disposed to assume "that there are no political tensions that cannot be resolved through sophisticated technocracy" (Oakley et al., 2006, p. 3) (Figure 4.2).

The extent to which this "surrender" occurs depends on country context. Even in the supranational case of the EU, the assumption of supranational control over the national economy of a country such as Greece was significant (Becker, 2017; Patomäki, 2017), and doubly so given the fact that the Greeks no longer had their own instruments including a national currency to adjust (Varoufakis, 2016). Certain IMF interventions in Latin America and Africa would be comparable in scope to that witnessed in Greece under the EU (Vreeland, 2003; Danaher, 2011; Woods, 2014; Widmaier, 2014). Indeed, it has been argued that the scale of devastation (public value destruction) wrought by the surrender of operational resources to both the EU and IMF by Greece and Argentina, respectively, would be comparable in terms of persistence and magnitude (Varoufakis, 2016; Moosa & Moosa, 2019a, 2019b).

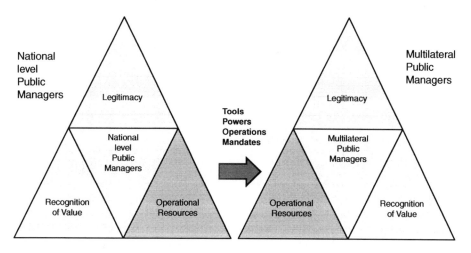

Figure 4.2 Surrender of operational resources to multilateral public managers.
Source: Author's research; see also Chohan (2019b).

In addition, there is the question of how the IMF's operational resources themselves are being deployed. As with other Bretton Woods institutions, the IMF's endowments are generally shrinking due to the lack of sustained operational support from the key stakeholders (Fratianni & Pattison, 2005; Rapkin & Strand, 2006). In recent years, the largest vote-holding country, the United States, has cut its development contribution substantially, with a particular focus on slashing its contributions to large multilateral development agencies including the IMF (Saldinger, 2019). The insistence is now being laid on "other countries paying their fair share" (Saldinger, 2019), and if not, then US taxpayers must not be the ones shouldering the lion's share of the burden. Furthermore, politicians in the United States have articulated their fear that if the United States does not act like a "tough guy," to put it in colloquial terms, in its engagements at multilateral institutions, then other countries will "take the US taxpayer for a ride" (Lee, 2002, p. 289; see also Fratianni & Patterson, 2005; Peet, 2009). This raises the legitimate concern about the resources of one public being used to fund the publics (including their politicians and public managers) of other countries, for perhaps insufficient return. This observation has also been made in the case of the supranational EU public, where the divergent priorities, endowments, and dispositions of various publics makes the imbalances between them perhaps too large to reconcile through a supranational mechanism (Chohan, 2019, p. 50). The consequence of this is that multilateral agencies themselves face considerable and tightening constraints in their operational resources. Therefore, rather than developing countries leading the charge against the IMF and World Bank based on the adverse effects of their policies on these societies (Woods, 2003; Barro & Lee, 2005; Blustein, 2003, 2006; Varoufakis, 2016), it is in fact the developed countries which are shrinking the operational resources of institutions which they themselves have used as instruments against the economies of the developing world (Danaher, 2011, Moosa & Moosa, 2019c).

Multilateral PV problems

Leadership of a world-public

It has long been recognized in the PV literature that the leadership of public managerial institutions plays an immense role in the direction of the initiatives that institutions take (Wallis & Gregory, 2009). By that account, it is necessary to understand the leadership structure of the IMF. In large part, it is framed by the voting rights of capital (see detailed review in Fratianni & Pattison, 2005; Rapkin & Strand, 2006) and so the richest contributing countries have the largest vote in dictating policy for an organization which is meant to bail out countries which are generally not very rich. As Dresner describes it, "power within the IMF is based on quota size, calculated using a complex formula of economic variables," such that today, and certainly prior to the 2008 Financial Crisis, "the allotment of quotas in the IMF bore little resemblance to the distribution of [world] economic power" (2012, p. 17). While there is a democratic element in instating the votes based on the amount of funding contributions, there are invariably many political consequences of such a leadership structure in policy formulation, and the voting structure of the IMF is thus a significant reason for its distortionary behavior (see Fratianni & Pattison 2005; Rapkin & Strand 2006).

Moreover, the structure of leadership at the IMF (as well as the other Bretton Woods institutions) represents the state of the world economy immediately after World War 2, a period that followed more than 300 years of European colonization. As some (but by no means all) formerly colonized countries have gained a relative measure of prosperity and spearheaded public value-creation efforts since independence, the arrangement of the IMF does not, for the most part, reflect their increased economic strength. In fact, the countries that have developed the most (e.g. China) since the end of colonialism and post-World War 2 are the ones that have most scrupulously avoided and ignored IMF prescriptions (see Barro & Lee, 2005; Blustein, 2006).

As Lee notes, "historically, a 'gentleman's agreement' between the Americans and (western) Europeans had seen a European assume the role of Managing Director at the IMF," while an American held the World Bank's presidency. This has come to generate a fear in the international public about representation and power – about who creates value for whom. As Lee remarks, "the attendant danger has been that the future role of the IMF will be largely determined by US unilateralism, rather than multilateral cooperation and genuine dialogue with IMF client states, let alone NGOs and other representatives of civil society" (2002, p. 288). This raises the important question of when civil society organizations might have a stake and voice in the implementation of programs for an international public, since PVT accords civil society with the status of being one of three main agents in public value co-creation (see Alford & O'Flynn, 2009; Benington, 2009).

Whether the IMF will itself play a leadership role in the global economy is also coming into question, given the aforementioned discussions on its declining operational resources, the diminishing recognition of its public value, and its legitimacy as an international financial institution. One thing to observe is that IMF staff, the human public managers behind the multilateral institution, are conspicuously absent from reform proposals (Momani, 2007). In fact, rival institutions are beginning to crop up around the world, particularly in China where substitutes for Bretton Woods institutions such as the Asian Infrastructure Investment Bank (AIIB) or the BRICS Bank (Brazil, Russia, India, China, South Africa) have begun to lend to developing countries with fewer political stipulations and less intrusion into the structure of the public (see Chohan, 2018a, 2018c). The success of such new institutions in public value creation might encourage them to take a leadership position in international development over time, for as Benington remarks, public value is an approach that evaluates meaningfully over the longer-term (2009, p. 240). The Bretton Woods institutions have had 75 years to enforce their leadership over the world-public, and given the diversity of outcomes (but the persistence of a large Global South), there is ample room to suggest that their multilateral public managerial leadership is likely to diminish with time.

Rhetoric

Alford and O'Flynn (2009) had highlighted a criticism of PVT in the guise of rhetoric, since public managers could use PV as a legitimating device to strengthen their power (see budgetary example in Chohan & Jacobs, 2018). PVT would then be a convenient trick for public managers to frame their "praetorian usurpation" of power in the benign language of "value creation" (Wanna & Rhodes, 2007). When applied to the context of multilateral public managers, it appears that the IMF might exemplify the use of this rhetorical enterprise against the countries where it implements structural reforms (Peet, 2009; Danaher, 2011; Woods, 2014), and thus corroborate Wanna and Rhodes' critique (2007). It has indeed been found through empirical studies (see review in Barro & Lee, 2005) that the IMF often stalls growth and has a somewhat negative effect on the rule of law and democracy (Vreeland, 2003; Barro & Lee, 2005). Or as Moosa and Moosa frame it more emphatically, "if the IMF is judged by the declared objectives of eradicating poverty, boosting growth, enhancing social expenditure and raising the standard of living, then it has been a dismal failure," but by the same token, "if it is judged by the undeclared objectives of looting domestic assets, impoverishing developing countries, imposing neoliberal ideas on developing countries and having free access for the corporate 'west' to sources of raw materials and markets, then it has been a spectacular success" (Moosa & Moosa, 2019c, p. 165).

The rhetoric that the IMF applies involves the lexicon of "development," "stability," and "economic growth." According to its own statements, the IMF is "a cooperative of 185 member countries, whose objective is to promote world economic stability and growth," and which aims to provide its members with "macroeconomic policy advice, financing in times of balance of payments need, and technical assistance and training to improve national economic management" (Fritz-Krockow & Ramlogan, 2007, p. 1). It uses the collaborative language that would resonate with PV theorists who urge for the co-creation of public value (Moore, 2003), as when Article 1 of the IMF declares that it shall "promote international monetary cooperation through a permanent institution which provides the machinery for consultation and collaboration on international monetary problems" (Fritz-Krockow & Ramlogan, 2007, p. 1). It also uses the benign language of a contributor and facilitator who is helping countries to realize their potential, as when it aims "to contribute to the promotion and maintenance of high levels of employment and real income and to the development of the productive resources of all members as primary objectives of economic policy" (Fritz-Krockow & Ramlogan, 2007, p. 7). Finally, its greatest deviation in praxis from lofty rhetoric may be found in Article 1 which stresses that the IMF will strive "to correct maladjustments in [countries'] balance of payments without resorting to measures destructive of national or international prosperity" (Fritz-Krockow & Ramlogan, 2007, p. 7).

This rhetoric is repeated by national-level politicians in countries that seek reciprocal legitimation from the IMF. They insist that the IMF's savvy policies are international best practices that can salvage their economies and bring them up to par with the world's most dynamic countries. The reciprocal legitimation of these politicians by the IMF is such that the Fund issues press statements highlighting the "reform-oriented," "pragmatic," and "progressive" approach of pliant politicians (Blustein, 2003). As perhaps its most memorable example, before Argentina's economic collapse in 2001, the neoliberal president Carlos Menem was brought by the Fund to speak about the "miracle" of Argentina that followed IMF prescriptions (see narrative in Blustein, 2003, 2006), only to offer muted commentary that focused on rescue after the Argentine system stalled entirely. Because of the discrepancy between the rhetoric of their claims and the praxis of their policy implementation (Barro & Lee, 2005; Blustein 2003, 2006; Peet, 2009; Danaher, 2011), the IMF offers an interesting international PV example of the application of rhetoric by public managers that risks the possibility of usurping democratic mandates and public value destruction.

Value destruction

Spano asserts that when agents make poor choices that do not favor the public, the outcome may be "public value destruction" (2009, p. 335). This chapter has repeatedly alluded to the multilateral problem of just whose values are being reflected in multilateral institutions, and toward whom these values are being directed. Naturally, this subsumes the question of value destruction: do multilateral public managers become a conduit for the imposition of the values of one national public over another? Given the voting structure of the IMF and its domination by a few developed countries, the values that will most vociferously be articulated in IMF policymaking will be those of these developed countries (Fratianni & Pattison, 2005; Rapkin & Strand, 2006; Saldinger, 2019). Yet the ultimate recipients of IMF programs are developing countries in economic distress, which means that the values of certain rich countries will be made manifest in poorer countries, without their adequate representation in the voting structure of the IMF (Saldinger, 2019). Benington had argued that "public value" can be seen in two ways: first, what the public values; and second, what adds value to the public sphere (2009, p. 233). There are two implicit arguments embedded in the application of this statement to the IMF. First, the IMF might not adequately incorporate the values of the publics on whom it imposes programs; and second, its policies might not deliver economic growth and thus not add value to the public sphere.

The phenomenon of public value destruction is quite evident in the critiques of the IMF's policies regardless of the framework of analysis from which they derive. A straightforward socioeconomic inquiry has correlated the policies of the IMF with "riots and civil unrest" (Moosa & Moosa, 2019b, p. 89), citing incidences of "IMF riots" as mentioned earlier. More empirical approaches (see review in Barro & Lee, 2005) find that the IMF often stalls growth and has a somewhat negative effect on the rule of law and democracy (Vreeland, 2003; Barro & Lee, 2005). Although accusations are now being hurled at new IMF rivals such as the Chinese initiatives of Asian Infrastructure Investment Bank (AIIB) and the One Belt One Road (OBOR), for germinating "debt traps" (see review in Chohan 2018a, 2018c), it is in fact the IMF which was first identified as the modern perpetrator of debt traps in the developing world (Payer, 1975). Indeed, unlike the exploration of this chapter on the IMF, public value approaches show that OBOR is a meaningful surplus recycling mechanism as well as a means to "create public value between nations" (Chohan, 2019b, pp. 95–109). Conflating the performance of traditional multilateral institutions with that of newer institutions is therefore an important mistake to avoid in the examination of PV creation at the multilateral level.

When the IMF's policies lead to excessive PV destruction, there is a normal tendency to engage in blame-shifting exercises, with the Fund blaming national politicians and public managers for failing to adhere appropriately to its stipulated conditions, and national politicians accusing the IMF of betraying the public and demanding impossible outcomes that misled them (Woods, 2003; Blustein, 2003, 2006; Peet, 2009; Danaher, 2011). This speaks to Wallis and Gregory's insight that PV destruction is accompanied by a blame-shifting aspect that stems from the difference between *managerial accountability* and *political accountability* (2009). But as the section on the strategic triangle in this chapter has highlighted, the national-level politicians and politicians surrender operational resources to multilateral public managers, which means that although they face part of the blame from the public (and thus political accountability), they are in a weaker position to create value on their own terms while they face IMF conditionalities. At the same time, since the IMF does not adhere to adequate transparency and accountability in its own operation, it does not fulfill the PV aspect of managerial accountability as theorized by Wallis and Gregory (2009). As public managers, then, the staff and leadership of the IMF must consider what public value-creating role the Fund can play in the future, mindful of its shortcomings in the past. These are to be discussed in the concluding section.

Conclusion

It may be surmised from the foregoing discussions that there are severe limitations to the value creation of multilateral public managerial institutions. They are in fact reminiscent of the PV problems of supranational entities (such as the EU, see Chohan, 2019b, pp. 40–61), but dire and accentuated by an order of magnitude. For this reason, propositions regarding the PV creation of supranational institutions were transposed onto the multilateral case of the IMF, and the findings suggested that indeed, the problems of supranational PV creation resonated with the multilateral context, but they were worse largely due to the sheer size of the "public" in question (185 member countries in the IMF), the greater degree of intrusion by the IMF into the structure of economies, and the state of distress in which most countries turned to the IMF for bailouts. It was proposed that the diversity of national publics in the world made it nigh-on-impossible to reconcile the contradictory and competing values of divergent publics at different stages of development. It was also proposed that the IMF is not bound by national-level democratic arrangements, and so does not feel beholden to any specific public for transparency or accountability. In terms of the articulation of values, the IMF's constituent voter base being largely dominated by a handful of wealthy countries' voting shares has meant that they articulate their perspectives and values most visibly in the policymaking structures of multilateral institutions.

From the perspective of national-level politicians and public managers, it was proposed using Moore's strategic triangle that in times of reliance on IMF bailouts and structural adjustment programs, they surrendered operational tools to the IMF in order to adhere to the stipulations and conditionalities of bailout programs. This reduced their value-creation abilities and bound them to a responsibility even when IMF programs hampered or destroyed value. They remained accountable to the public despite having fewer operational resources to act on the public's behalf, even as the IMF was not accountable to any public per se. In the end, this might lead to a loss of trust between the public and IMF, between politicians and the IMF, and between the public and politicians too. In instances of severe value destruction, this would also lead to a blame-shifting exercise that pinned these agents against one another, with condemnatory rhetoric flowing between agents. Rhetoric itself, it was argued, is exemplified as a public managerial strategy by the IMF, given the disparities between its stipulated aims and the policies that it implements. Its leadership role in international value creation is thus stymied and this impacts its legitimacy and any recognition of the value it otherwise creates for the world-public.

As such, there is in fact a great deal of civil society and academic voice behind abolishing the IMF (Danaher, 2011), and as a former economist at the Financial Institutions Division of the Bureau of Statistics at the IMF laments, "it is to be concluded that, given the damage that has been inflicted on developing countries by following IMF-prescribed policies over many years, the option of maintaining the status quo is a non-starter" (Moosa & Moosa, 2019c, p. 135). Danaher presents ten reasons to abolish the IMF (2011), while other authors offer fewer but more precise reasoning for either its transformation, reformation, or abolition. Meynhardt has observed that in PVT, "legitimization by numbers may appear a less complex challenge than facing the challenge of a pro-active dialogue about 'why our work is valuable to society'" (2009, p. 214). Reformist advocates of the IMF plead that "as a future alternative to expensive public bailouts with their attendant risk of moral hazard, the emphasis in IMF activity should be upon 'bail-ins' that involve the private sector in the prevention, management and resolution of financial crises" (Lee, 2002, p. 287). In public value terms, this reduces the direct role of multilateral public managers in crisis management by roping in the private markets.

Since public value itself does not directly encapsulate private interest (see Chohan, 2018b), but recognizes the dominance of neoliberalism's market emphasis, such a reformist proposal might fit within PV's argumentation, but this requires future research. Another reformist approach toward a suggested solution involves the creation of still more multilateral institutions. As Lee has framed it,

> among the proposals for reform have been the establishment of an International Credit Insurance Corporation (ICIC) and the creation of a Tobin Tax Organization to act as a counterweight to the IMF and World Bank as part of a democratisation and politicisation of the global governance.
> (2002, p. 287)

Others mentioned earlier in the chapter include those tied to Chinese international development (Chohan, 2018a, 2018c) including the Asian Infrastructure and Investment Bank (AIIB) or the BRICS Bank for deployment in BRICS nations (Brazil, Russia, India, China, South Africa).

The IMF was an important financial institution in the heyday of globalization, and it promoted policies that were conducive to the integration of national publics into the world-public from a market-oriented perspective. Globalization itself has come to be challenged due to the value destruction that is perceived by members of the public in many countries (Stiglitz & Pike, 2004; Margalit, 2012). Citizens are articulating anti-globalist values and emphasizing the importance of their publics as meriting preservation and protection, and national-level politicians and public managers are responding to these values through a variety of strategies (Stiglitz and Pike, 2004; Margalit, 2012). This includes an increased repudiation (barring the extreme need for an economic bailout) of the IMF and other Bretton Woods institutions. They are attempting to seize back the operational resources surrendered to globalist institutions over the years, and are challenging the legitimacy of these institutions while questioning outright the value-contribution of these institutions (Stiglitz & Pike, 2004; Margalit, 2012).

To deal with the growing backlash and changes in the values of the public, multilateral public managers can adopt several lessons taught in PVT. First, the public managers who work inside these institutions must have a greater say in the policy development process. Second, the voting structure and leadership of the IMF and similar institutions must be revisited and altered to make them more inclusive and representative of the world-public. Third, these institutions must respond proactively to the values articulated by citizens of poorer publics, and work more in unison with national-level public managers and politicians. Fourth, they must build a coalition of sufficient support for their activities among the publics they engage with. Fifth, they must reconsider the degree of constraints they impose on, and operational resources they seize from, national-level PV agents. Sixth, they must deploy a greater value-seeking imagination in executing value-creating strategies at a time of backlash against globalization. Seventh, they must pay closer attention to the need for civil society participation in multilateral fora. It is only by following such lines of action that multilateral public managers can do justice to the important mandates they have had in the world, and serve the wider public of the world which they were created to serve.

References

Ahamed, L. (2014). *Money and Tough Love: On Tour with the IMF.* London: Visual Editions.

Alford, J., & O'Flynn, J. (2009). Making Sense of Public Value: Concepts, Critiques and Emergent Meanings. *International Journal of Public Administration, 32*(3–4), 171–191.

Barro, R. J., & Lee, J. W. (2005). IMF Programs: Who Is Chosen and What Are the Effects?. *Journal of Monetary Economics, 52*(7), 1245–1269.

Beck Jorgensen, T., & Vrangbaek, K. (2011). Value Dynamics: Towards a Framework for Analyzing Public Value Changes. *International Journal of Public Administration, 34*(8), 486–496.

Becker, J. (2017). In the Yugoslav Mirror: The EU Disintegration Crisis. *Globalizations, 14*(6), 840–850.

Benington, J. (2009). Creating the Public in Order to Create Public Value? *International Journal of Public Administration, 32*(3–4), 232–249.

Benington, J., & Turbitt, I. (2007). Policing the Drumcree Demonstrations in Northern Ireland: Testing Leadership Theory in Practice. *Leadership, 3*(4), 371–395.

Blustein, P. (2003). *The Chastening: Inside the Crisis That Rocked the Global Financial System and Humbled the IMF*. Washington, DC: Public Affairs.

Blustein, P. (2006). *And the Money Kept Rolling In (and Out) Wall Street, the IMF, and the Bankrupting of Argentina*. Washington, DC: Public Affairs.

Chohan, U. W. (2018a). The Political Economy of OBOR. In J. Chaisse & J. Gorski (Eds.), *The Belt and Road Initiative: Law, Economics, Politics* (pp. 59–82). Netherlands: Brill Nijhoff.

Chohan, U. W. (2018b). *The Roles of Independent Legislative Fiscal Institutions: A Multidisciplinary Approach*. (Doctoral Thesis), University of New South Wales (UNSW), Canberra.

Chohan, U. W. (2018c). What Is One Belt One Road? A Surplus Recycling Mechanism Approach. In J. Chaisse & J. Gorski (Eds.), *The Belt and Road Initiative: Law, Economics, Politics* (pp. 205–219). Netherlands: Brill Nijhoff.

Chohan, U. W. (2019a). The FATF in the Global Financial Architecture: Challenges and Implications. *Monetary Economics: International Financial Flows, Financial Crises, Regulation & Supervision eJournal: Social Science Research Network (SSRN), 19*(1), 1–34.

Chohan, U. W. (2019b). *Public Value and Budgeting: International Perspectives*. London: Routledge.

Chohan, U. W., & Jacobs, K. (2018). Public Value as Rhetoric: A Budgeting Approach. *International Journal of Public Administration, 41*(15), 1217–1227.

Constable, S., Passmore, E., & Coats, D. (2008). *Public Value and Local Accountability in the NHS*. London: NHS.

Danaher, K. (2011). *10 Reasons to Abolish the IMF & World Bank*. London: Seven Stories Press.

Douglas, S., & Meijer, A. (2016). Transparency and Public Value: Analyzing the Transparency Practices and Value Creation of Public Utilities. *International Journal of Public Administration, 39*(12), 940–951.

Dresner, D. (2012). The Irony of Global Economic Governance: The System Worked. *Tufts University Papers: Fletcher School of Law & Diplomacy*.

Fratianni, M., & Pattison, J. (2005). Who is Running the IMF: Critical Shareholders or the Staff? In P. de Gijsel & H. Schenk (Eds.), *Multidisciplinary Economics* (pp. 279–292).Boston, MA: Springer.

Fritz-Krockow, B., & Ramlogan, P. (2007). *International Monetary Fund Handbook: Functions, Policies, and Operations*. Washington, DC: IMF.

Graeber, D. (2015). *The Utopia of Rules*. Brooklyn, NY: Melville House.

Künneth, W., & Beyerhaus, P. (1975). *Reich Gottes oder Weltgemeinschaft: Die Berliner Ökumene-Erklärung zur utopischen Vision des Weltkirchenrates*. Berlin: Bad Liebenzell: Verlag der Liebenzeller Mission.

Lee, S. (2002). The International Monetary Fund. *New Political Economy, 7*(2), 283–298.

Lowndes, V., Pratchett, L., & Stoker, G. (2006). Local Political Participation: The Impact of Rules-in-use. *Public Administration, 84*(3), 539–561.

Margalit, Y. (2012). Lost in Globalization: International Economic Integration and the Sources of Popular Discontent. *International Studies Quarterly, 56*(3), 484–500.

Meynhardt, T. (2009). Public Value Inside: What Is Public Value Creation? *International Journal of Public Administration, 32*(3–4), 192–219.

Momani, B. (2007). IMF Staff: Missing Link in Fund Reform Proposals. *The Review of International Organizations, 2*(1), 39–57.

Moore, M. (1994). Public Value as the Focus of Strategy. *Australian Journal of Public Administration, 53*(3), 296–303.

Moore, M. (1995). *Creating Public Value: Strategic Management in Government*. Cambridge, MA: Harvard University Press.

Moore, M. (2003). *The Public Value Scorecard. A Rejoinder and an Alternative to "Strategic Performance Measurement and Management in Non-Profit Organizations" by Robert Kaplan* Hauser Center for Nonprofit Organizations Working Paper, 18.

Moore, M., & Khagram, S. (2004). *On Creating Public Value: What Business Might Learn from Government about Strategic Management*. John F. Kennedy School of Government, Harvard University.

Moore, M. (2014). Public Value Accounting: Establishing the Philosophical Basis. *Public Administration Review, 74*, 465–477.

Moore, M., & Donahue, J. (2012). *Ports in a Storm: Public Management in a Turbulent World*. Cambridge, MA: Harvard University.

Moore, M., & Khagram, S. (2004). *On Creating Public Value: What Business Might Learn from Government about Strategic Management*. Cambridge.

Moosa, I. A., & Moosa, N. (2019a). The Effects of IMF Operations on Social Expenditure. In *Eliminating the IMF* (pp. 111–134). Cham: Palgrave Macmillan.

Moosa, I. A., & Moosa, N. (2019b). The IMF as an Instigator of Riots and Civil Unrest. In *Eliminating the IMF* (pp. 89–110). Cham: Palgrave Macmillan.

Moosa, I. A., & Moosa, N. (2019c). Keep, Reform or Abolish? In *Eliminating the IMF* (pp. 135–163). Cham: Palgrave Macmillan.

Oakley, K., Naylor, R., & Lee, D. (2006). *Giving Them What They Want: Constructing the 'Public' in Public Value*. London: BOP Consulting.

Patomäki, H. (2017). Will the EU Disintegrate? What Does the Likely Possibility of Disintegration Tell about the Future of the World? *Globalizations, 14*(1), 168–177.

Payer, C. (1975). *The Debt Trap: The International Monetary Fund and the Third World* (Vol. 376). New York: NYU Press.

Peet, R. (2009). *Unholy Trinity: The IMF, World Bank and WTO*. London: Zed Books.

Rapkin, D. P., & Strand, J. R. (2006). Reforming the IMF's Weighted Voting System. *World Economy, 29*(3), 305–324.

Saldinger, A. (2019, 12 March). US Budget Slashes Global Development Funding, Stresses Burden Sharing. *Devex*.

Samaratunge, R., & Wijewardena, N. (2009). The Changing Nature of Public Value in Developing Countries. *International Journal of Public Administration, 32*(3–4), 313–327.

Spano, A. (2009). Public Value Creation and Management Control Systems. *International Journal of Public Administration, 32*(3–4), 328–348.

Stiglitz, J., & Pike, R. M. (2004). Globalization and Its Discontents. *Canadian Journal of Sociology, 29*(2), 321–340.

Stoker, G. (2006). Public Value Management: A New Narrative for Networked Governance?. *American Review of Public Administration, 36*(1), 41–57.

Stone, R. (2003). *Lending Credibility: The International Monetary Fund and the Post-Communist Transition*. Princeton, NJ: Princeton University Press.

Talbot, C. (2009). Public Value—The Next "Big Thing" in Public Management? *International Journal of Public Administration, 32*(3–4), 167–170.

van der Waal, Z., & van Hout, E. T. (2009). Is Public Value Pluralism Paramount? The Intrinsic Multiplicity and Hybridity of Public Values. *International Journal of Public Administration Review, 32*(3–4), 220–231.

Varoufakis, Y. (2016). *And the Weak Suffer What They Must? Europe's Crisis and America's Future*. New York: Nation Books.

Vreeland, J. R. (2003). *The IMF and Economic Development*. Cambridge: Cambridge University Press.

Wallis, J. (2010). A Tale of Two Leaders: Leadership and Cultural Change at the New Zealand Treasury. *Australian Journal of Public Administration, 69*(1), 22–33.

Wallis, J., & Gregory, R. (2009). Leadership, Accountability and Public Value: Resolving a Problem in "New Governance"?. *International Journal of Public Administration, 32*(3–4), 250–273.

Wanna, J., & Rhodes, R. (2007). The Limits to Public Value, or Rescuing Responsible Government from the Platonic Gardens. *Australian Journal of Public Administration, 66*(4), 406–421.

Widmaier, W. (2014). From Bretton Woods to the Global Financial Crisis: Popular Politics, Paradigmatic Debates, and the Construction of Crises. *Review of Social Economy, 72*(2), 233–252.

Wiegratz, J. (2016). *Neoliberal Moral Economy: Capitalism, Socio-cultural Change and Fraud in Uganda*. London: Rowman & Littlefield.

Williams, I., and Shearer, H. (2011). Appraising Public Value: Past, Present and Futures. *Public Administration, 89*(4), 1367–1384.

Woods, N. (2003). Order, Justice, the IMF, and the World Bank. In J. L. G. A. H. Rosemary Foot (Ed.), *Order and Justice in International Relations* (pp. 112–131). Oxford University Press.

Woods, N. (2014). *The Globalizers: The IMF, the World Bank, and Their Borrowers*. Ithaca, NY: Cornell University Press.

Chapter 5

Central banks as public managers

Introduction

The aim of this chapter is to delve into the nature of central banks as institutions of non-traditional public managers (NTMs), with a view to teasing out some of the most interesting nuances that surround their work from a public value perspective. As with other chapters in the book, this one also follows a propositional method, and the propositions are summarily presented in Table 5.1. The structure of the chapter is set as follows. First, it will discuss the modes of value creation by central banks, bifurcating this into the two ambits of monetary policy and financial supervision. The section will stress how the value-creating role of the central bank has been critiqued and also changed since the 2008 Global Financial Crisis (GFC). Second, it will discuss aspects of the politics–administration dichotomy and public value in politics (Roberts, 1995; Chohan, 2017a; Chohan & Jacobs, 2017b, 2018) as they materialize in central banks. This is an issue of interest given that the role of administration in monetary affairs is resurfacing as a salient debate (Hayo & Hefekker, 2010; Ueda & Valencia, 2014; Fels, 2016). In addition, some heed is paid to nuances around the roles of political and administrative power in monetary emission and supervision.

Next, the chapter considers the arbitration of value in monetary terms, including the response to the articulation of values by citizens. Fourth, the chapter highlights a peculiar aspect of central bank value creation in that they set the price of money, which means they influence the mode by which value is ascribed to a great many (but certainly not all) things that the public values, thus impacting the value-choices of citizens to some degree. Fifth, a discussion is presented about "public value and rhetoric" (see Chohan & Jacobs, 2018) and how the statements of central bankers can in fact adjust the expectations of the public regarding the exercise of value creation, as when Federal Reserve (Fed) statements are carefully monitored for their language and their signaling regarding the future path of the economy. These notions are offered a degree of synthesis regarding central bankers as non-traditional managers (NTMs) in the concluding section.

Table 5.1 Propositions on central banks

Number	Proposition
1	Central banks create value in two ambits: monetary policy and financial supervision. They address citizen values regarding financial stability, employment, and inflation, and economic growth. Both ambits have changed somewhat since the Global Financial Crisis (GFC) of 2008.
2	Central banks enjoy far more independence than other public managers do, and this offers certain benefits (monetary de-politicization) and certain challenges (democratic accountability) in terms of politics-administration dichotomy.
3	Central banks co-create value, but do not respond directly to political or citizen exigencies. They may even override citizen and political demands, which challenges notions of the arbitration of value.
4	Central banks set the price of money through interest rates, and so influence the medium through which citizens ascribe value to many (but not all) things.
5	The rhetoric of central banks regarding the economic trajectory can actively shape citizen and politician expectations about the future; while also acting as a barrier to active political involvement in monetary policy.

Source: Author's research.

There are three important caveats that warrant emphasis at this juncture. First, as Balls et al. succinctly put it: "no single country has yet settled the question about how a modern central bank should be structured" (2016, p. 4), which is why this chapter seeks to avoid making general and normative suggestions about how central banks *should be* designed when looking at them through the lens of public value. Second, the chapter looks at national-level public managers at central banks, not supranational ones such as the European Central Bank (ECB), because the dynamics of supranational central banking require considerable elaboration beyond the scope of a single chapter, and are likely to find consonance with the study of PV creation by supranational entities (see Chohan, 2019, pp. 40–61). That said, the chapter does consider coordination among national-level central banks for international financial stability (see public value "between nations" in Chohan, 2019, pp. 95–109). Third, over the years there has emerged such a rich body of work on central banks, and from so many divergent perspectives, that no chapter-length treatment of the PV of central banks could ever do justice to subject; this must be acknowledged before the chapter makes a humble attempt that is mindful of the vastness of the economic literature on central banks as a whole.

It is also worth remarking that although they are described as non-traditional managers (NTMs) in this book because of the absence of deep PV-oriented treatments of monetary authorities, central banks themselves are in fact quite an old stock of public manager. After all, the Bank of England was established in 1694 and the Bank of France in 1800 (Elgie & Thomson, 2002), and the Swedish and Dutch banks even earlier. Furthermore, considerable shifts have taken place over history with respect to the relationship that the preponderant structures of central government maintain with monetary authorities, as, for example, when Cahan et al. remark that "the relationship between government ideology and monetary policy has varied greatly over time, often because of structural changes in the global economic environment," and also that "a great deal of heterogeneity exists between countries" (2019, p. 1).

Similarly, Elgie and Thomson observe that "the relationship between governments and central banks has been subject to great variation over time," but that "the politics of monetary policy has become increasingly complex and national governments appear to be losing control over monetary policy," which means that "core issues concerning the political control of economic life are as salient as ever" (Elie & Thomson, 2012, p. 1). Given their pivotal role in any discussion of political control of economic life, the chapter highlights the fact that central banks *can* offer exceptional insights into public value creation due to their unique positioning within the architecture of public administration.

The value creation of central banks

Central banks form a pillar of market economies and often aim to attain several goals by striking appropriate balances between key variables. As such, the value-creating activities of central banks may be summarily bifurcated into two co-mingled categories: monetary policy and financial stability. We may frame this as the first proposition of this chapter:

> *Proposition 1: Central banks create value in two ambits: monetary policy and financial supervision. They address citizen values regarding financial stability, employment, and inflation, and economic growth. Both ambits have changed somewhat since the Global Financial Crisis (GFC) of 2008*

However, in suggesting a division into two ambits, the degree of overlap between both categories should be emphasized, not just in the tools, but also in the outcomes of policies executed. For example, the GFC of 2008 demonstrated the need not just for stimulating economic activity after a market panic, but also for calm and reassurance through the re-imposition of a stable environment for international finance (Peters et al., 2011; Dresner, 2012; Corder, 2014). Indeed, the multiplicity and hybridity of central bank goals speaks to Public Value Theory's (PVT) recognition of multiplicity and hybridity in values that complicates the public manager's ability to address them (see van der Waal & van Hout, 2009), particularly since there may be

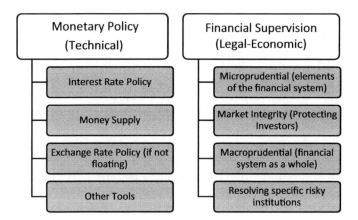

Figure 5.1 Categories of central bank value creation.
Source: Restoy (2018), Balls et al. (2016), Peters et al. (2011); Author's research.

competing or conflicting elements between those values (Chohan & Jacobs, 2018). The two categories of central bank value creation are depicted visually in Figure 5.1.

The first category of monetary policy is the traditional ambit of central banks, and it involves the application of tools such as interest rate policy, money supply, and exchange rate policy, along with certain less conventional tools (and while working with the formal banking system), to manage rates of inflation, unemployment, and liquidity while fostering economic growth (see Kydland & Prescott, 1977; Sargent & Wallace, 1981; Barro & Gordon, 1983; Rogoff, 1985; Havrilesky, 1987; Walsh, 1995; Issing, 2011; Dincer & Eichengreen, 2014; Cahan et al., 2019). Financial stability involves the oversight and supervision of financial markets, the banking sector, and non-bank financial institutions (NBFIs) using some of the same tools as in monetary policy, but more so through mechanisms that are rather legal-structural than they are economic in nature (see De Haan & Van't Hag, 1995; Geraats, 2002; Dresner, 2012; Buiter, 2014; Corder, 2014; Balls et al., 2016; Fels, 2016).

Meanwhile, the second category of central bank value creation, financial supervision, involves several considerations, and Restoy has classified them as consisting of four functions; two of which are somewhat traditional, while two others have emerged largely in the wake of the GFC of 2008 (Restoy, 2018). The two traditional functions are as follows: the oversight of financial institutions as elements within the financial system (microprudential), and the protection of investors through market integrity. The two more recent components are: monitoring of the financial system as a whole (macroprudential), and "the resolution of vulnerable banks able to generate systemic stress" (Restoy, 2018, p. 1), i.e. dealing with specific crisis-afflicted entities. The latter two became extremely important functions after the jolts of the 2008 GFC led governments to realize that the overall stability of the system required careful attention, and specific risks (such as particularly troubled institutions) would require immediate remedial actions (Dresner, 2012).

As Balls et al. remark, "prior to the financial crisis, a consensus had developed around the model of an ideal central bank: independent from government, with a focus on price stability through an inflation target, with primary responsibility for moderating macroeconomic fluctuations" (2016, p. 5). Over time, the central banks of both developed and developing countries came to converge upon this model of central bank independence (CBI), but the other roles of central banks, notably the supervision of financial markets and the maintenance of macroeconomic stability, were increasingly handed over to other agencies. The logic behind this was that the value creation of central banks would have been maximized by focusing on its responsibilities in monetary policy (see also Balls et al., 2016, p. 5).

However, according to Restoy, central banks have "gained competences in financial oversight" since the GFC, such that they are now the prudential supervisor for banks and non-bank financial institutions (NBFIs) in many developed-country jurisdictions (2018, p. 4), and are now both the resolution authority (for troubled institutions) as well as macroprudential authority for 60% of such jurisdictions (Restoy, 2018). Indeed, one space where central bank PV value has been recognized has been in the coordination between central banks to help stem global crises, such that "despite initial shocks that were actually more severe than the 1929 financial crisis, global economic governance structures responded quickly and robustly" (Dresner, 2012).

However, there is some debate as to whether central banks should be allowed to act as *sole* supervisors of the financial regulatory architecture, or whether a cohort of government agencies (i.e. institutions of public managers) should collectively oversee different aspects of the overall architecture (see Dresner, 2012; Dincer & Eichengreen, 2014; Balls et al., 2016; Restoy, 2018). As public value recognizes (Stoker, 2006; Chohan, 2018), such functions are the subject of difficult tradeoffs. In this particular case, it has been framed as follows: on the one hand, central banks can "exploit synergies across different functions by grouping them within a specific authority," but on the other, they must then consider their ability "to minimize conflicts across objectives" which could be better addressed by having different institutions (Restoy, 2018, p. 5). As an example, one might take the conflict between maintaining solvent banks (microprudential) and protecting the interests of customers (market integrity). Indeed, historically the fact that central banks were largely staffed by economists, even in their supervisory divisions, meant that central banking praxis reflected an orientation toward monetary policy rather than financial supervision (Goodhart et al., 2002). A seminal study of the aptitudes of central bankers by Goodhart et al. revealed that the economist bent was widespread in the supervisory department where a legal and compliance orientation would have perhaps been more appropriate (2002).

To which of the central bank's objectives do citizens ascribe the most value: lower unemployment, lower inflation, market stability, currency stability, economic growth, or market integrity? Balls et al. observe that "social preferences about financial stability are often less clearly defined and first-order distributional effects are likely to be greater than with conventional monetary policy" (2016, p. 4). This is why, from the traditional application of social welfare functions (see Hayo & Hefekker, 2010; Corder, 2014), it is difficult to state in PV terms what the degree of acceptable tradeoff is between one aspect of central bank value creation and the other, and as Balls et al. note, "it is very difficult, for instance, to set up a welfare function that allows the central bank to optimise the trade-off between economic dynamism and financial stability" (2016, p. 3).

Central bank independence and the politics-administration dichotomy

In delineating the monetary policy and financial supervisory roles of central banks, it should be remarked that they have generally proceeded with their value-creation efforts while enjoying a significant degree of independence and autonomy (Hayo & Hefekker, 2010; Dincer & Eichengreen, 2014; Ueda & Valencia, 2014; Fels, 2016), whether it be in setting policy goals, in evading direct political intrusion, or in the choice of policy instruments. As Cahan et al. observe, "governments do not design monetary policies directly in industrialized countries: central banks do," but government may still "influence monetary policies indirectly by, for example, appointing politically aligned members to the central bank council or signaling preferred policies" (Cahan et al., 2019; see also Chappell et al., 1993). The degree of central bank independence (CBI) varies between countries (de Haan & vant Hag, 1995, p. 336), but so too do the *forms of independence* that central banks enjoy, as listed in Table 5.2 (see also Hayo & Hefekker, 2010; Ueda & Valencia, 2014; Balls et al., 2016; Fels, 2016).

Goal independence regards the central bank's ability to set its own policy goals, which is akin to articulating its own values, and then decide how they shall be pursued. Typical examples of goal independence in the monetary policy area might include a central bank setting its own inflation target (usually for "2% inflation"), setting a fixed exchange rate (whether relative to a specific country or to a basket of currencies), or the control of money supply (e.g. currency in circulation or in banking reserves). From a public value perspective, this would in theory be regarded as a very strong form of public manager independence relative to politicians, in that the public managers can establish their own parameters of operation. In practice, however, goal independence is still adjoined to a negotiating process (see also PV

Table 5.2 Forms of central bank independence

Form	Description
Goal Independence	A central bank can set its own policy goals such as inflation targeting, fixed exchange rate, and control of money supply. It can then be held accountable for its achievement of those goals, and also negotiate goals with government.
Functional/ Operational Independence	A central bank can choose its policy instruments / modes of achieving value creation objectives, along with the resource types (staff, budgets). This is the most common type.
Institutional Independence	A central bank's independence is enshrined into law, protecting it from direct political intrusion and keeping its mandate outside the political realm.

Source: Ueda and Valencia (2014), Fels (2016), Hayo and Hefekker (2010), Balls et al. (2016).

negotiation in Moore, 1995), whereby central banks give and take cues from government about which goals require the most active pursuit. This confers two PV advantages: first, it allows for a degree of transparency, in that central banks can then be held to account by politicians for the degree of achievement of stipulated goals; and second, it might allow for public managers and politicians to come to greater agreement about what values are articulated by citizens. Nevertheless, goal independence can also mean that central banks can pursue their own agendas and thus exemplify the PV critique of "public value in politics" (see Alford & O'Flynn, 2009; Chohan, 2017b; Chohan & Jacobs, 2017b).

Functional/operational independence, in PV terms refers to a central bank's ability to choose the operational resources necessary to attain stipulated goals, including the staff, expertise, budgets, and other operational aspects including programs, databases, and equipment. Having functional independence is, however, not the same as goal independence, since the values which are to be pursued are articulated by politicians instead. Functional independence has been found to be the most common form of CBI around the world (De Haan & Van't Hag, 1995; Hayo & Hefekker, 2010), in part because it is the least demanding from a politics-administration dichotomy perspective (see Chohan, 2017a, p. 1009), but also because it allows the input of politicians and the rest of government to direct the pursuit of objectives while leaving it to the technical expertise of central bankers to execute policy objectives (see also Corder, 2014; Chohan, 2017b). An early example of such independence was the New Zealand monetary experiment, whereby the Reserve Bank of New Zealand would pursue goals that were set from above but had discretion in approaching the goals using tools of its choice (Dowd & Baker, 1994).

Institutional independence regards the separation of central banks from the domain of direct political intrusion, usually through the formal enshrinement of a central bank's independence into law, or otherwise through a very significant amount of informal disassociation between central banks and politics (de Haan & vant Hag, 1995, p. 340). The concept goes both ways: politicians are deemed extraneous to monetary policy (but not financial supervision), and central banks are barred from an overtly political role. Through institutional independence, there lies "a minimal risk that central banks interpret their mandate too widely and wade into larger debates about inequality, fiscal policy and other 'political' issues outside of their remit" (Buiter, 2014, p. 4). Institutional independence varies significantly between countries. For example, in the United States, the Federal Reserve ("Fed") operates under a premise of remarkable independence from direct political interference. In fact, the first central bank to be made so independent was the Bundesbank of Germany (Dowd & Baker, 1994; De Haan & Van't Dag, 1995). In many countries, however, the central bank is not institutionally independent and is instead placed under the executive branch through constitutional provisions (see Latin American examples in Wang, 2016). However, the institutional independence of a central bank can change over time, especially when the independence is not (fully) formally enshrined.

For example, Corder remarks that "as recently as 1949, the Fed was simply an administrative agent for the Department of the Treasury" and so was "under the strict political control of the president and his cabinet," and yet "thirty years later, the Chairman of the [Fed], Paul Volcker, committed the central bank to a series of monetary policy choices that produced a serious recession," leaving Corder to ask: "how does a federal agency undergo such a transformation, from subordinate to autonomous, in less than thirty years?" (2014, p. 3). For many decades now, "the Fed [has been] exempt from the appropriations process, and opportunities for appointment of key Fed actors is rare," even though "structure of the Fed and statutory language describing the instruments of monetary policy are quite similar to language incorporated into the Federal Reserve Act in 1935" (Corder, 2014, p. 16). From a PV standpoint, institutional independence is the most à propos to the question of the politics–administration dichotomy (see Roberts, 1995; Chohan, 2017a, p. 1009), because it resonates with the inherent tension that public administration faces in confronting the questions where politicians are meant to the "final arbiters of value" (Moore, 1995, p. 38).

This allows for the postulation of a second proposition in this chapter:

Proposition 2: Central Banks enjoy far more independence than other public managers do, and this offers certain benefits (monetary de-politicization) and certain challenges (democratic accountability) in terms of politics-administration dichotomy

In terms of independence, Balls et al. note that "prior to the financial crisis, a consensus had developed around the model of an ideal central bank: *independent from government*" (2016, p. 5, emphasis added). Another pillar of this consensus was the belief, demonstrated in much theoretical and empirical economic research that a central bank would be more effective at controlling inflation without significantly impacting economic growth or unemployment, so long as it was structured as an *independent institution*. The language used to justify this expertise (see also "public value as rhetoric" in Chohan & Jacobs, 2018) was of *technical expertise*, which speaks to what critics of public value theory deride in PVT that it pretends "that there are no political tensions that cannot be resolved through sophisticated technocracy" (Oakley et al., 2006, p. 3). As Corder notes, "central bank policy makers exploited technical sophistication and other information asymmetries to foreclose meaningful political oversight" (2014, p. 4).

The prime merit of CBI was argued to lie in protecting monetary instruments from direct and excessive political manipulation to finance a deficit economy, including avoiding the politically engineered business cycle where governments would go on spending binges before elections to gain votes (Buchanan & Wagner, 1977; Sargent & Wallace, 1981). Rogoff (1985) and Walsh (1995) had argued that CBI could help overcome the *time-inconsistency problem* described by Kydland and Prescott (1977) and Barro and Gordon (1983), whereby governments could have a strong motivation to boost economic numbers in the short-run through unexpected demand shocks, which might reduce unemployment but inefficiently raise long-term inflation.

Yet even when the Fed was at its peak in terms of independent influence over the American economy, a series of studies (see review in Corder, 2014) still indicated that the Fed was responsive to American politics (see also example in Havrilesky, 1987). Stalwart central bankers, such as Alan Greenspan, have themselves made this argument, noting that they had the best intentions for value co-creation with politicians but ultimately struggled with issues of "the map and the territory," referring to the shorthand of monetary tools at their disposal (their operational resources), which didn't square up with the complex and interdependent nature of global economic life (Greenspan, 2013). Although there are some groups of economists who argue that the notion of CBI is somewhat exaggerated (see Alt, 1991, p. 43), it is perhaps useful to note that "the relationship between government ideology and monetary policy has varied greatly over time, often because of structural changes in the global economic environment" (Cahan et al., 2019); and because of this, papers written in some periods will point to moderate CBI while others will identify excessive CBI.

But why would powerful politicians, both in the executive and legislature, allow for CBI to reach such an extent? After all, "inaction may be attractive for strategic and informed legislators under [only] a fairly limited set of conditions" (Corder, 2014, p. 4). One reason is that the Fed "exploited technical sophistication and other information asymmetries" and reinforced an aura of complexity that portrayed the intimidating nature of the macroeconomy

(Krugman, 2011; Corder, 2014, p. 4); a kind of "central bank voodoo" to dissuade politicians from engaging with monetary policy (see Krugman, 2011). This speaks to Oakley et al.'s criticism of PVT's lax attitude toward apolitical technocracy (2006). However, Corder explores three other intriguing hypotheses: first, that "the Fed may be a useful scapegoat for macroeconomic failures" (Corder, 2014, p. 4); and second, that Congress in fact does exercise much influence, but it is tacit.

Corder's third hypothesis, however, is the most intriguing in that it suggests that Congress benefits systematically from CBI in its power relative to the executive branch (Corder, 2014; see also *presidentialisation thesis* in Chohan & Jacobs, 2017a). It can do so because CBI prevents executive exertion over monetary affairs, while Congress itself can "can independently develop new federal credit institutions to protect narrow segments of financial markets from Fed choices" (2014, p. 4). This would suggest a unique PVT interplay between politicians and bureaucrats (see also "Politicians v. Bureaucrats" in Chohan, 2017b) because in the antagonistic legislative-executive design of presidential systems (or even parliamentary systems that are becoming increasingly presidential, see review in Chohan & Jacobs, 2017b), two political institutions can engage in a tussle through the medium of central banks without exerting direct influence over the central bank itself. Therefore, Corder surmises that CBI is "a joint product of the strategic actions of Fed decision makers and the desire of members of Congress to frustrate executive control over monetary policy outcomes" (2014, p. 130).

However, CBI has always been met with some degree of distrust in the economics literature, perhaps most prominently when framed through the Marxian prism, as when Greider once remarked that "some observers of the American political economy lament the formal subordination of representative democracy to the demands of owners of capital" (Greider, 1987, p. 3). After the 2008 GFC, questions about CBI resurfaced as a major arena of intellectual contention. Balls et al., for example, remark that "as these unelected, technocratic, institutions become increasingly powerful, the pre-crisis academic consensus around central bank independence – put crudely, 'the more, the better' – has become inadequate" (2016, p. 3). Furthermore, they note that the act of crisis management, as exemplified in the GFC 2008, is by its very nature a political enterprise, stressing that "the government should lead crisis management efforts because this area is inherently political and contentious, it is difficult to codify ex-ante processes and accountability mechanisms and, finally, it involves the coordination of multiple agencies" (Balls et al., 2016, p. 4; see also Geraats, 2000; Dincer & Eichengreen, 2014).

For developing countries specifically (see PVT in developing countries in Samaratunge & Wijewardena, 2009; Chohan, 2019, pp. 21–40), there is the additional dynamic that emerges from interactions with large global multilaterals such as the International Monetary Fund (IMF) (see also the previous chapter on multilaterals). Recent research suggests that the IMF exerts considerable influence on international CBI efforts for "ulterior motives" including the de-politicization of its emergency packages and the aim of establishing "a politically insulated veto player to promote its economic policy reform agenda" (Kern et al., 2019, p. 212). This represents an example of external intrusion into the domestic value-creation processes of a public with a view to establishing stronger public managers but doing so at the expense of politicians, who would be the final arbiters of value in a democratic society. Contrastingly, the Federal Reserve is compared to the IMF in the GFC 2008 context as a true "lender of last resort" when financial markets go haywire, along with the accompanying "politics of rescuing the world's financial system" (Broz, 2015, p. 323). In both developed and developing countries, then, there is an issue of "public value in politics" (Chohan & Jacobs, 2017b) as it concerns central banks and their relationship to politicians, with concomitant questions of central bank accountability, which are discussed in the following section.

The arbiters of value?

The foregoing discussion raises questions about the accountability of central banks as unelected officials with considerable power over economic life. Peters et al. caution that the challenge of governance that we face is the lack of co-creation of value as caused by "the fragmentation of the state, both horizontally and vertically" (2011, p. 2). The absence of co-creation has "contributed to the inability of governments to monitor effectively and to regulate effectively," and they attribute this to the logic of governance that has underpinned the structures for the past several decades, which "has been to divide the public sector into numerous single-purpose organizations," with the ostensible purpose of enhancing the efficiency of service delivery (2011, p. 2). This compartmentalization, however, "also has tended to divide information and regulatory powers, and therefore limited the capacity of the public sector to understand and regulate risk," while ideological biases (read: neoliberalism) have "blinded governments to the real possibilities of economic failures coming from markets with inadequate supervision" (Peters et al., 2011).

As Balls et al. remark, "there are also concerns that it is too difficult to hold central banks democratically accountable for their new powers [post-2008]" (2016, p. 3; see also Issing, 2011). They add that

> shifting power away from the political process to independent institutions is, by its nature, undemocratic. It should only be done both when there are large benefits to removing the decision-making from the political process and when it is relatively easy to hold the independent institution accountable for its decisions.
>
> (2016, p. 4)

As with other NTMs, this requires what Lowndes et al. call the "renewal of citizen consent" (2006, p. 552), and what Benington and Turbitt term the "coalition of sufficient support" that must be forged to generate legitimacy in the eyes of the public (2007, p. 383). Furthermore, when central banks set their own targets (such as inflation targeting), their performance can be gauged ex-post facto against these targets, which offers another form of accountability (Geraats, 2000; Dincer & Eichengreen, 2014).

Yet putting monetary policy aside, scholars have observed that the ambit of financial supervision is much more elusive for such feedback-oriented accountability to be imposed. As Balls et al. comment, "in financial policy, however, it is much more difficult to set up effective accountability mechanisms," in no small part because "'financial stability' is more difficult to define than price stability ('2% inflation')," but also that "the tools to achieve it, such as macroprudential measures, are less well understood than conventional monetary policy tools such as interest rates" (2016, p. 12). It may be further noted that the complex nature of global economic connectivity allows financial actors to engage in *regulatory arbitrage*, bouncing between jurisdictions to suit their private interests. This makes it even more "difficult to delineate ex-ante the necessary toolkit to tackle risks to financial stability" (Balls et al., 2016, p. 12).

This permits for the assertion of a third proposition in this chapter:

> *Proposition 3: Central Banks co-create value, but do not respond directly to political or citizen exigencies. They may even override citizen and political demands, which challenges notions of the arbitration of value*

From a PVT perspective, there is a looming question on renegotiating the central bank's space in its authorizing environment, with greater emphasis on the values articulated by citizens. However, "social preferences about financial stability are often less clearly defined and first-order distributional effects are likely to be greater than with conventional monetary policy" (Balls et al., 2016, p. 4), which is to say that there is an ambiguity about the degree to which citizens ascribe value to financial stability, and so central public managers face the challenge in degree to which this value must be accommodated. Financial stability is in essence a public good (see also *public* goods in previous chapters of this book). As Balls et al. frame the conundrum, "it is very difficult, for instance, to set up a welfare function that allows the central bank to optimise the trade-off between economic dynamism and financial stability" (2016, p. 3). But there is one step further in the politics-administration, and it is articulated thus:

> As a central bank becomes increasingly powerful, then, it may seek to impose its preferences on society. If the government has no control over the objective, personnel or other sources of leverage, it cannot influence

the central bank when it disagrees with the latter's model of the economy or when it prioritises different issues.

(Balls et al., p. 2)

Politicians unable to exert direct agency over so core an area of economic life thus face a conundrum as final arbiters of value, even as "the expansion in central bank powers over the last few years has placed these institutions at the heart of many contentious economic problems" (Balls et al., 2016; see also Varoufakis, 2016; Graeber, 2019). The post-2008 economic climate has been riddled with disappointing economic trajectories in the developed world, and at least partial blame for this has been laid on the shoulders of central banks for their recalcitrance to act appropriately (Corder, 2014; Taylor, 2014; Balls et al., 2016; Graeber, 2019). Many scholars increasingly assert that if the public managers sitting in independent central banks are unwilling to stimulate their economies, then politicians in elected governments should reassume control of monetary policy, and that the public value-creation exercise should once again be driven by political means (Issing, 2011; Buiter, 2014; Balls et al., 2016).

To take the point still further, Restoy highlights the growing argument that central bank monetary policies have in some instances represented more of a fiscal regime, as when "purchasing large amounts of public debt in secondary markets as part of their quantitative easing [QE] programmes," which was "de facto performing a quasi-fiscal function" (Restoy, 2018, p. 4). There is a political-fiscal element to this because those policies have had "significant distributional effects across different segments of the population" (Restoy, 2018,p. 4; see also Taylor, 2014; Graeber, 2019). Yet there appears "to be currently a higher social sensitivity to possible unintended distributional effects of public policies which may have some influence on the public debate on [CBI]" (Restoy, 2018; see also Issing, 2011; Buiter, 2014). In essence, central banks do not take signals directly from citizens, and they do not constitute a class of politicians who would normally serve as the conduit for the articulation of values in a democratic society (Moore, 1995; Chohan & Jacobs, 2017a; Chohan, 2019). The recognition of this issue offers an opportune occasion to deploy Moore's strategic triangle (1994, 1995), the "central symbol" of public value (Alford & O'Flynn, 2009, p. 173), vis-à-vis central banks.

Strategic triangle for central banks

Premised on the discussion of the previous two sections, we may examine central banks through the three nodes of Moore's strategic triangle: legitimacy, recognition of value, and operational resources (see Moore, 1995). They are presented summarily in Table 5.3.

Table 5.3 The strategic triangle for central banks

Form	Description
Legitimacy	Central banks across both developed and developing countries have enjoyed various degrees of independence and of legitimacy. The space of economic neutrality, reputation as technical experts, and various forms of independence that central banks have enjoyed for many decades is increasingly coming into question, as politicians and citizens post-GFC 2008 seek to understand the value proposition of central banks as unelected officials spearheading monetary policy and financial supervision.
Recognition of Value	Each aspect of central bank value creation is recognized separately for its contribution. In (developed country) monetary policy, inflation has been curbed, but unemployment and economic growth are increasing concerns. In financial supervision, central bank coordination has been forthcoming, but microprudential and macroprudential risks remain, and whether just one institution should take charge of financial supervision is still debatable.
Operational Resources	Operational independence is the most common form of CBI, and central banks have picked from their toolkits to resolve various parameters in monetary policy and financial supervision. In general, central bank operational resources are greater now than before the GFC, but there is a great deal of variety among countries. Operational resources might be constrained by the public's future choices to reduce CBI.

Source: Ueda and Valencia (2014), Fels (2016), Hayo and Hefekker (2010), Balls et al. (2016).

Legitimacy

Trust and legitimacy are argued to be the "eventual goal of public value" (Talbot, 2009, p. 168), and as a very first point on legitimacy, it should be noted that the legitimacy of central banks varies across countries (de Haan & vant Hag, 1995, p. 337). It is then worth recalling that prior to the GFC, there was an increasing consensus on the ideal form of a central bank, which conferred significant CBI and heightened legitimacy for central bank primacy in monetary policy and financial supervision (Balls et al., 2016). The legitimacy of central banks rested in no small part on their occupation of technical expertise and a "space of economic neutrality" (Lebaron, 2000, p. 208), and on their reputations as stable and apolitical organizations (Greenspan, 2013). Reputation had always been central to the effective function of central banks (Barro & Gordon, 1983), because their credibility would help determine the degree to which they would impact and direct financial systems. Political (and especially legislative) representatives tolerated this preeminence of central banks in the monetary sphere for several suggested reasons (Corder, 2014; see also de Haan & vant Hag, p. 1995), including a possible scapegoat, a vehicle for tackling other political elements (legislative vs. executive), or indeed because they did continue to exercise sufficient power.

The reputations and legitimacy of central banks, however, took a very serious dent after the GFC of 2008 (Dresner, 2012; Greenspan, 2013), and the re-establishment of credible institutional repute has been a priority for public managers at central banks around the world. Since the GFC, Restoy remarks that

> despite the analytical appeal of the integration of financial sector responsibilities within the central bank, the accumulation of [so much] power within a single agency may pose issues of *political legitimacy* which could end up being resolved by introducing excessive constraints on central banks' mandates and operational procedures.
>
> (2018, p. 4, emphasis added)

Furthermore, "in the wake of the global financial crisis, the [traditional] model of a central bank is being challenged," and in the United States, Congress "only narrowly rejected" Senator Rand Paul's "Audit the Fed" plan to curtail the Federal Reserve's independence, which would have "significantly curtailed Fed independence by requiring the Fed to set interest rates according to a predefined rule" (Balls et al., p. 4; see also fiscal rules in Chohan, 2017c) and would have subjected the Fed's monetary policy decisions to constant congressional review. Beyond the United States, politicians in other countries have also begun to question the independence of central banks, including in the United Kingdom, Chile, Iceland, India, Brazil, and many others (Corder, 2014; Balls et al., 2016; Restoy, 2018; Graeber, 2019). Even mainstream academic voices have begun evoking "long-held taboos such as monetary financing of governments" (otherwise known as *helicopter money*), and have questioned how valuable central bank independence really is (Krugman, 2011; Corder, 2014; Balls et al., 2016; Restoy, 2018; Graeber, 2019).

To address the question of their public value legitimacy, and given the forms of CBI discussed earlier, Balls et al. advise that central banks in advanced economies might "sacrifice some *political* independence without undermining the operational independence that is important in both their monetary policy and financial stability functions" (2016, p. 3). In any case, the likelihood of a rearrangement of powers in the monetary and financial supervision ambits of many advanced economies is increasing, and some reinforcement of politicians as "final arbiters of value" (Moore, 1995, p. 38), true to PVT, is being advocated, at least for crisis situations such as the GFC of 2008 (Balls et al., 2016; Restoy, 2018). PVT recognizes that "legitimization by numbers may appear a less complex challenge than facing the challenge of a proactive dialogue about 'why our work is valuable to society'" (Meynhardt, 2009, p. 214), and the problem that central bankers face in seeking sustained legitimacy for their work as public managers is that politicians and civil society have begun to demand clearer answers about how central bankers create value and how they respond to the values articulated by citizens. This speaks to PVT's appeal that there is a need to "rebuild public confidence in political institutions, and the most powerful way to do that is to seek active citizen endorsement of the policies and practices of public bodies" (Stoker, 2006, p. 48).

Recognition of value

Certainly, there are forms of central bank public value creation that have been (and are still being) given due recognition, despite the heightened alertness to the role of central banks and to the consequences of having unelected officials at the heart of the monetary system. For example, the Bank for International Settlements (BIS) acknowledged in its 2012 annual report that "decisive action by central banks during the global financial crisis was probably crucial in preventing a repeat of the experiences of the Great Depression" (BIS, 2012, p. 39). As Dresner observes, "whether one measures results by economic outcomes, policy outputs, or institutional flexibility, global economic governance has displayed remarkable resiliency since 2008" (2012, p. 4). In terms of public opinion, according to the Pew Research Centre (2015), 47% of Americans polled had a favorable opinion of the Fed and 37% had an unfavorable opinion (Pew Research Centre, 2015). This could in fact be disaggregated by political affiliation to show that Republicans generally had a more mistrusting view (48% unfavorable) than Democrats did (28% unfavorable) (Pew Research Centre, 2015).

However, for the major central banks, which enjoyed considerable independence in the past, there are increasing questions about the politics-administration dichotomy and the final arbiters of value in monetary policy and financial supervision. Because of this, "absolutist interpretations of complete central bank independence may both undermine the pursuit of new central bank objectives and fray the political support that currently exists for central bank autonomy in their core monetary policy function" (Balls et al., 2016). To put it more plainly, "popular discontent towards central banks is growing in the US, UK and the euro-zone," not to mention in emerging markets, and "the backdrop of weak recoveries in many countries is likely to exacerbate the political impact of the problems" (Balls et al., 2016, p. 3; see also Krugman, 2011; Varoufakis, 2016; Graeber, 2019).

In another example, much theoretical and empirical pre-crisis work showed that so long as certain conditions exist and CBI is assured, central banks in advanced economies would generally do well at managing inflation (see review in earlier section). Yet the problem of inflation now seems to be an increasingly outdated one, which is why central bank focus must also be laid on unemployment and on stimulating growth. In advanced economies, the traditional tools appear to be more hampered (zero-bound interest rates, continuous stimulus packages), while unconventional tools are increasing but the justification of their use is still being debated (Balls et al., 2016; Restoy, 2018). On the financial supervision side, central banks are recognized as important institutions, but micro- and macroprudential risks remain, and whether just one institution should take charge of financial supervision is still debatable (Buiter, 2014; Balls et al., 2016). Therefore, as with legitimacy, the recognition of central bank value is also facing shifts that are inspired by citizen and politician reconsideration of the permissibility of CBI.

Operational resources

The introductory section of this chapter offered a rudimentary overview of the types of operational resources and tools that central banks use for monetary policy and financial supervision. The monetary ambit includes not only traditional tools such as interest rate policy and money supply control but also a greater number of unconventional tools (such as quantitative easing, QE). The financial supervision ambit uses some tools similar to monetary policy, but mainly consists of elements that are legal-structural in nature. For both value-creating ambits, the general observation has been that central banks have gained more powers since the 2008 financial crisis, but the types of powers are different from country to country (Taylor, 2014; Fels, 2016), reflecting therein the "a substantial divergence in central banks' goals, tools and institutional structures," along with other operational resources (Balls et al., 2016).

Although, the monetary success of post-crisis advanced economies continues to be debated, Dresner offers the argument that central banks have been using their operational resources well and in coordination with one another: "from the earliest stages of the financial crisis, there was also concerted and coordinated action among central banks to ensure both discounting and countercyclical lending" (Dresner, 2012, p. 13; see also fiscal coordination in Chohan & Jacobs, 2016). This also involved the use of unconventional tools, and so "not content with lowering interest rates, most of the major central banks also expanded other credit facilities and engaged in more creative forms of quantitative easing" even to the extent that for the period 2007–2012, "the balance sheets of the central banks in the advanced industrialized economies more than doubled" (Dresner, 2012, p. 13).

Yet as the discussion of the other two nodes (legitimacy and recognition of values) reveals about central banks today, there are concerns about giving central banks such a breadth of operational resources without adequate accountability. The *forms of independence* conferred on central banks might therefore be revisited in countries around the world where politicians and citizens are beginning to express doubts about the conferral of generous operational resources, tools, and mandates, without adequate democratic representation in the process. Combining all three nodes of the triangle therefore suggests that although central banks are recognized as a core pillar of market economies, the degree to which they can act with independence in driving value-creation is likely to be revisited due to a general shift in the public's perception regarding the role of these public managers in creating value for society.

Measuring the value of value

There is a philosophical element to the question of how "value" is ascribed by the public in PVT that might best be explored through the lens of central banks. Central banks determine the value, or more precisely, the *price*, of money (Kydland & Prescott, 1977; Greider, 1987; Walsh, 1995), and money is a medium for the public to ascribe value to a broad swathe of elements in public life (Graeber, 2012). Central banks control the price of money through interest rate and money supply policies, since an interest rate determines the base return for money over time (its value in investment; see Graeber, 2012), while the supply of money determines how much currency is allowed in circulation (Rogoff, 1985; Greenspan, 2013). In capitalist societies with a strong market-orientation, such as those for which PVT was designed (Moore, 1995; Moore and Khagram, 2004; Benington, 2009), money is a primary (but not the sole) medium for the determination of value. This means that central banks influence the "value" of the medium through which things are valued. Central banks are public managers uniquely positioned to ascribe value to the medium of value itself, and this permits a fourth proposition:

> *Proposition 4: Central Banks set the price of money through interest rate and money supply policies, and so influence the medium through which citizens ascribe value to many (but not all) things*

In other words, money is a common medium of exchange through which the public can express the value that it ascribes to many (but certainly not all) things in society. Putting this proposition into praxis, a central bank can make money itself cheaper or dearer as a part of its approach to addressing the values addressed by the public (e.g. lower unemployment, lower inflation, economic growth, etc.). However, this shouldn't be taken to mean that PVT emphasizes an excessive market-logic in its public managers, since PVT urges public managers to go beyond "narrow monetary outcomes to include that which benefits and is valued by the citizenry more generally" (Williams & Shearer, 2011, p. 1367; see also Moore & Khagram, 2004). By raising interest rates or tightening the money supply, central banks can make money itself more valuable, with less money chasing the same number of goods and services in society. Conversely, by lowering interest rates or loosening the money supply, central banks can make money less valuable, with a greater amount of money slushing around and chasing the same number of goods and services. Since the GFC of 2008, the value of money in developed economies has generally been cheapened through lower interest rates and excess supply (Peters et al., 2011; Taylor, 2014; Fels, 2016), and central bankers have been reticent to make money dearer in the decade since.

Yet even as interests have gradually and only slightly gone up since the GFC in developed countries, central banks in the developed world are failing to generate economic growth and are not facing the inflationary pressures their traditional models would have predicted. Indeed, any attempts to stimulate growth, be it through shrinking interest rates (even in negative real interest rate terms) or through flooding the money supply, now fail to generate inflation in developed markets (Hayo & Hefeker, 2010; Dincer & Eichengreen, 2014; Balls et al., 2016; Fels, 2016). On this point, Restoy has argued that "the absence of an immediate inflation threat has made the traditional arguments that supported the case for central bank independence in the academic literature somewhat less influential in the current policy debate" (2018, p. 3). This has led an increasing number of economists to recommend the pursuit of "new solutions to new problems" (Peters et al., 2011).

The "value" in PVT can itself be categorized in two ways according to Benington (2009, p. 233): first, what the public values; and second, what adds value to the public sphere. The argument of this section is that there is a third aspect of value categorization in PV, in that a specific type of public manager can ascribe value to the medium of value (money), thereby making the medium of translating value more or less valuable in order to pursue other values articulated by the public. In this sense, central banks constitute a non-traditional manager (NTM) category in PVT that is not merely a passive agent receiving signals about the values of the public, but is exerting a measure of agency in shaping the values of citizens by determining the value of the primary medium of value. This reframing of public manager agency, as shaping the value of value, is one that requires much further debate in the PV discourse, for while there is the traditional expectation of public managers taking cues from citizens and politicians in co-creating value, there are in fact fundamental ways in which public managers can shape the values of citizens by framing the mechanisms through which citizens ascribe measurable monetary value to their values.

The rhetoric of central banks

Central bankers offer a certain embodiment of the PVT problem known as "public value and rhetoric," but in a different guise from that traditionally understood (Alford & O'Flynn, 2009; Chohan & Jacobs, 2018). The issue of rhetoric in PVT is generally meant to refer to the risk that public managers might use PV as a rhetorical legitimating device to usurp power from politicians (Wanna & Rhodes, 2007; Alford & O'Flynn, 2009). However, there are two other interesting aspects of rhetoric for PV that are reflected in central banks: first, they use their technical and abstruse language to keep political interference at bay (Krugman, 2011; Greenspan, 2013; Corder, 2014, p. 4); and second, that their rhetoric can actually influence the public's expectations about the future path of the economy (Waud, 1970; Greider, 1987; Romer & Romer, 2000; Aizenman et al., 2014; Broz, 2015). This may be presented as a fifth proposition in this section, as follows:

Proposition 5: The rhetoric of central banks regarding the economic trajectory can actively shape citizen and politician expectations about the future; while also acting as a barrier to active political involvement in monetary policy

For the first aspect, it is important to note that the technical expertise that central banks exude in the monetary policy domain involves the application of a certain economic jargon that appears abstruse to politicians and certainly to the public (Geraats, 2000; Greenspan, 2013; Corder, 2014). This creates a barrier to more active political involvement in central bank activities as well, since research suggests that politicians do not have the same grasp of the monetary lexicon/rhetoric that expert central bankers do (see Buiter, 2014; Corder, 2014; Chohan, 2018). This barrier, in turn, exacerbates the politics–administration dichotomy, since politicians face a challenge in policy intercession without a grasp of the proper rhetoric that governs monetary policy (Krugman, 2011). Rhetoric is thus a device for the legitimation of central bankers (see also Wanna & Rhodes, 2007), but not in the sense of deploying public value itself. Rather, it frames the work of monetary policy decision-making as too abstruse for either the public or their elected representatives to directly engage with it (Krugman, 2011; Corder, 2014; Graeber, 2019). For comparison, this problem is much less acute in the ambit of financial supervision, which also explains why in various countries (Dresner, 2012, p. 13; Taylor, 2014; Fels, 2016), financial supervision is managed either outside of the central bank or in cooperation between the central bank and other public manager institutions.

For the second aspect, it is worth noting that a central bank's rhetoric, as expressed in its correspondence, minutes, and announcements, has an impact on the public's expectations of future value creation because it sets the tone for the central bank's outlook in future periods (Waud, 1970; Greider, 1987; Romer & Romer, 2000; Aizenman et al., 2014; Broz, 2015). This is a phenomenon long recognized in the economics literature, as when Waud described the Fed's "announcement effect," noting that it had a "psychological impact on the public's expectations" (1970, p. 231). Greider describes this ominously as part of "the secrets of the temple" in the Fed's influence over public life through its mere signaling (1987), while Romer and Romer highlight the asymmetry of information between the public and the Fed which leads individuals to "modify their forecasts in response to those signals" that are disseminated by the central bank (2000, p. 429). The world-public (see also the previous chapter on multilaterals) is impacted by the rhetoric of powerful national central banks (most notably the US Fed), as demonstrated in the work of Aizenman et al., which illustrates how both robust and fragile emerging markets respond to the rhetoric of the Fed in its announcements regarding QE and interest rates (2014). The rhetoric of the "voodoo" central bank (Krugman, 2011) thus becomes a source of power over the public which, PVT would argue, must be exercised with responsibility, since it is this rhetoric which induces "public interpretation" (Waud, 1970, p. 231). Indeed, this is a manifestation of PV rhetoric that helps to solidify the PV strategic triangle elements of central banks as they proceed to inform the public about the economic possibilities and likelihoods of subsequent periods.

In sum, this section helps to show what future research must explore more keenly, and in various ways, regarding the rhetorical element in PVT; not just as an accusation against public managers for legitimizing their power grabs through PV mantras (Wanna & Rhodes, 2007; Chohan & Jacobs, 2018), but also through the aforementioned two rhetorical aspects: a technical jargon of inaccessibility that barricades political intrusion; and as a vehicle to actually shape the values of the public in future periods. To frame it more broadly, "public value as rhetoric" remains underexplored in that there are more nuanced types of rhetorical strategies, influences, gambits, and consequences that have yet to receive fuller consideration in the PV literature.

Conclusion

Central banks are a category of NTMs which help inform several aspects of PVT that require further attention, including the degrees of independence afforded to public managers, public value in politics, the articulation of values by citizens, the ascription of value by the public, and the impact of rhetoric on value creation. Each of these was given a degree of treatment in the various sections of this chapter, but further research must expand on the ideas presented, particularly regarding the questions of PV rhetoric and the measurement of value. For both of these issues, the chapter has emphasized that public managers can actively shape the values of citizens, whether by adjusting the price of the medium through which value is ascribed (e.g. QE), or through the announcement effect of central bank commentary. It is in fact curious that central banks had not been considered for more rigorous treatment in PVT earlier, but the thesis of this book is in fact that there are various types of non-traditional managers that have yet to receive due exploration through PVT lenses, so as to explain their predicaments (e.g. CBI) and also reciprocally to inform PVT's inquiry through those NTMs.

As for central bank public managers themselves, we must recall that "no single country has yet settled the question about how a modern central bank should be structured" (2016, p. 4), but the foregoing discussions of this chapter suggest that there may be a shift in CBI and in the three nodes of the strategic triangle in the coming years. As Balls et al. observe, "popular discontent towards central banks is growing in the US, UK and the euro-zone," not to mention in emerging markets, and "the backdrop of weak recoveries in many countries is likely to exacerbate the political impact of the problems" (2016, p. 3). The concern that certain authors raised long ago, about the extent of CBI in a democratic society, are coming to the fore, echoing what Greider once stated: "some observers of the American political economy lament the formal subordination of representative democracy to the demands of owners of capital" (Greider, 1987, p. 3). Graeber argues that

> there is a growing feeling, among those who have the responsibility of managing large economies, that the discipline of economics is no longer fit for purpose. It is beginning to look like a science designed to solve problems that no longer exist.
>
> (2019, p. 49)

The old value-creation paradigms and assumptions may be outdated, argues Graeber, and yet institutional thinking is not adapting,

> despite the fact that, since the 2008 recession, central banks have been printing money frantically in an attempt to create inflation and compel the rich to do something useful with their money, and have been largely unsuccessful in both endeavors.
>
> (2019, p. 50)

Indeed, while wealthy nations have been characterized by low inflation over the past two decades, there are other values such as shrinking real wages, sluggish economic growth, and unemployment that have been more pressing (Varoufakis, 2016; Chohan, 2018), which central banks are struggling to contend with under a new paradigm of urgency.

Some suggestions have been offered regarding the reworking of legitimacy and the revisitation of PV recognition for central banks. As but one example, Balls et al. recommend that "a coordination mechanism should be established" (2016, p. 3; see also Chohan & Jacobs, 2016), which involves "a body that is responsible for the oversight and prioritization of systemic risks to the financial system," with an emphasis on its engagement in value-seeking co-creation, involving "the central bank, other regulators and the government [with a] diverse membership [that] will minimize the dangers of group think and help coordinate responses to systemic risks." If such oversight bodies are created, they might help to address the issues raised in earlier sections while also emphasizing public value co-creation. Yet much more work is still required to understand the nature of value creation through powerful public managerial institutions that operate with considerable independence; and given the nature of complexity and interdependence, not to mention multiplicity and hybridity in public values, this chapter can offer but an introductory effort to stimulate those deeper PVT discussions that are yet to come.

References

Aizenman, J., Binici, M., & Hutchison, M. M. (2014). The Transmission of Federal Reserve Tapering News to Emerging Financial Markets. *National Bureau of Economic Research Working Papers No. 19980*.

Alford, J., & O'Flynn, J. (2009). Making Sense of Public Value: Concepts, Critiques and Emergent Meanings. *International Journal of Public Administration, 32*(3–4), 171–191.

Alt, J. (1991). Leaning into the Wind or Ducking Out of the Storm: U.S. Monetary Policy in the 1980s. In A. Alesina & D. Carliner (Eds.), *Macroeconomics and Politics in the 1980s*. Chicago: University of Chicago Press.

Balls, E., Howat, J., & Stansbury, A. (2016). *Central Bank Independence Revisited: After the Financial Crisis, What Should a Model Central Bank Look Like?* Cambridge, MA: Harvard Kennedy School.

Bank of International Settlements. (2012). *82nd Annual Report*. Switzerland: Bank of International Settlements.

Barro, R., & Gordon, D. (1983). Rules, Discretion, and Reputation in a Model of Monetary Policy. *Journal of Monetary Economics, 12*(1), 101–121.

Benington, J. (2009). Creating the Public in Order to Create Public Value? *International Journal of Public Administration, 32*(3–4), 232–249.

Benington, J., & Turbitt, I. (2007). Policing the Drumcree Demonstrations in Northern Ireland: Testing Leadership Theory in Practice. *Leadership, 3*(4), 371–395.

Broz, J. L. (2015). The Politics of Rescuing the World's Financial System: The Federal Reserve as a Global Lender of Last Resort. *Korean Journal of International Studies, 13*(2), 323–351.

Buchanan, J. M., & Wagner, R. M. (1977). *Democracy in Deficit*. New York: Academic Press.

Buiter, W. (2014). *Central Banks: Powerful, Political and Unaccountable?* (Discussion Paper No.10223). Centre for Economic Policy Research.

Cahan, D., Dörr, L., & Potrafke, N. (2019). Government Ideology and Monetary Policy in OECD Countries. *Public Choice, 181*(3–4), 215–238.

Chappell, H. W. Jr., Havrilesky, T. M., & McGregor, R. R. (1993). Partisan Monetary Policies: Presidential Influence through the Power of Appointment. *Quarterly Journal of Economics, 108*, 185–218.

Chohan, U. W. (2017a). Independent Budget Offices and the Politics-Administration Dichotomy. *International Journal of Public Administration, 41*(12), 1009–1017.

Chohan, U. W. (2017b). Public Value: Bureaucrats vs Politicians. In A. Farazmand (Ed.), *Global Encyclopedia of Public Administration, Public Policy, and Governance* (pp. 1–7) New York: Springer.

Chohan, U. W. (2017c). Qu'est-ce que une Charte d'honnêté budgetaire? Le cas d'Australie. *La Revue Parlementaire Canadienne, 40*(1).

Chohan, U. W. (2018). *The Roles of Independent Legislative Fiscal Institutions: A Multidisciplinary Approach*. (Doctoral Thesis), University of New South Wales (UNSW), Canberra.

Chohan, U. W. (2019). *Public Value and Budgeting: International Perspectives*. London: Routledge.

Chohan, U. W., & Jacobs, K. (2016). A Parliamentary Budget Office in Fiji: Scope and Possibility. *Australasian Parliamentary Review, 31*(2), 117–129.

Chohan, U. W., & Jacobs, K. (2017a). The Presidentialisation Thesis and Parliamentary Budget Offices. *Parliamentary Affairs, 70*(2), 361–376.

Chohan, U. W., & Jacobs, K. (2017b). Public Value in Politics: A Legislative Budget Office Approach. *International Journal of Public Administration, 40*(12), 1063–1073. doi: 10.1080/01900692.2016.1242612

Chohan, U. W., & Jacobs, K. (2018). Public Value as Rhetoric: A Budgeting Approach. *International Journal of Public Administration, 41*(15), 1217–1227.

Corder, K. (2014). *Central Bank Autonomy: The Federal Reserve System in American Politics*. London: Routledge.

De Haan, J., & Van't Hag, G. J. (1995). Variation in Central Bank Independence across Countries: Some Provisional Empirical Evidence. *Public Choice, 85*(3–4), 335–351.

Dincer, N. N., & Eichengreen, B. (2014). Central Bank Transparency and Independence: Updates and New Measures. *International Journal of Central Banking., 3*(3), 1–65.

Dowd, K., & Baker, S. (1994). The New Zealand Monetary Policy Experiment—A Preliminary Assessment. *The World Economy, 17*(6), 855–867.

Dresner, D. (2012). The Irony of Global Economic Governance: The System Worked. *Tufts University Papers: Fletcher School of Law & Diplomacy*.

Elgie, R. & Thomson, H. (2002). *The Politics of Central Banks*. London: Routledge.

Fels, J. (2016). *The Downside of Central Bank Independence*. New York: Pimco.

Geraats, P. M. (2000). Why Adopt Transparency? The Publication of Central Bank Forecasts. *CEPR Discussion Papers 2582*. Berlin: CEPR.

Geraats, P. M. (2002). Central Bank Transparency. *The Economic Journal, 112*(48), 532–535.

Goodhart, C., Schoenmaker, D., & Dasgupta, P. (2002). The Skill Profile of Central Bankers and Supervisors. *Review of Finance, 6*(3), 397–427.

Graeber, D. (2012). *Debt: The First 5000 Years*. London: Penguin.

Graeber, D. (2019). Against Economics. *New York Review of Books, 19*(47–69).

Greenspan, A. (2013). *The Map and the Territory: Risk, Human Nature, and the Future of Forecasting*. New York: Penguin.

Greider, W. (1987). *Secrets of The Temple: How the Federal Reserve Runs the Country*. New York: Simon and Schuster.

Havrilesky, T. (1987). A Partisanship Theory of Fiscal and Monetary Regimes. *Journal of Money, Credit and Banking, 19*(2), 308–355.

Hayo, B., & Hefeker, C. (2010). *The Complex Relationship between Central Bank Independence and Inflation*. In Challenges in Central Banking. Cambridge: Cambridge University Press.

Issing, O. (2011). *Lessons for Monetary Policy: What Should the Consensus Be?* Washington, DC: IMF Working Papers.

Kern, A., Reinsberg, B., & Rau-Göhring, M. (2019). IMF Conditionality and Central Bank Independence. *European Journal of Political Economy, 59*(1), 212–229.

Krugman, P. (2011, November 10). A Note on Hysterisis and Monetary Policy. *New York Times*.

Kydland, F., & Prescott, E. (1977). Rules Rather Than Discretion: The Inconsistency of Optimal Plans. *Journal of Political Economy, 85*(2), 473–491.

Lebaron, F. (2000). The Space of Economic Neutrality: Types of Legitimacy and Trajectories of Central Bank Managers. *International Journal of Contemporary Sociology, 37*(2), 208–229.

Lowndes, V., Pratchett, L., & Stoker, G. (2006). Local Political Participation: The Impact of Rules-in-use. *Public Administration, 84*(3), 539–561.

Meynhardt, T. (2009). Public Value Inside: What Is Public Value Creation? *International Journal of Public Administration, 32*(3–4), 192–219.

Moore, M. (1994). Public Value as the Focus of Strategy. *Australian Journal of Public Administration, 53*(3), 296–303.

Moore, M. (1995). *Creating Public Value: Strategic Management in Government*. Cambridge, MA: Harvard University Press.

Moore, M., & Khagram, S. (2004). *On Creating Public Value: What Business Might Learn from Government about Strategic Management*. Cambridge: John F. Kennedy School of Government, Harvard University.

Oakley, K., Naylor, R., & Lee, D. (2006). *Giving Them What They Want: Constructing the 'Public' in Public Value*. London: BOP Consulting.

Peters, B. G., Pierre, J., & Randma-Liiv, T. (2011). Global Financial Crisis, Public Administration and Governance: Do New Problems Require New Solutions?. *Public Organization Review, 11*(1), 13–27.

Pew Research Centre. (2015). *American Views of the Fed Depend on Their Politics*. Washington, DC: Pew Research Centre.

Restoy, F. (2018). *Central Banks and Financial Oversight*. Paper presented at the Fundación Ramón Areces, Madrid.

Roberts, A. (1995). "Civic Discovery" as Rhetorical Strategy. *Journal of Public Policy Analysis and Management, 14*(2), 291–307.

Rogoff, K. (1985). The Optimal Degree of Commitment to an Intermediate Monetary Target. *Quarterly Journal of Economics and Politics, 100*(4), 1169–1189.

Romer, C. D., & Romer, D. H. (2000). Federal Reserve Information and the Behavior of Interest Rates. *American Economic Review, 90*(3), 429–457.

Samaratunge, R., & Wijewardena, N. (2009). The Changing Nature of Public Value in Developing Countries. *International Journal of Public Administration, 32*(3–4), 313–327.

Sargent, T. J., & Wallace, N. (1981). Some Unpleasant Monetarist Arithmetic. *Quarterly Review, Federal Reserve Bank of Minneapolis, 5*(3), 1–17.

Stoker, G. (2006). Public Value Management: A New Narrative for Networked Governance?. *American Review of Public Administration, 36*(1), 41–57.

Talbot, C. (2009). Public Value—The Next "Big Thing" in Public Management? *International Journal of Public Administration, 32*(3–4), 167–170.

Taylor, J. B. (2014). The Role of Policy in the Great Recession and the Weak Recovery. *American Economic Review, 104*(5), 61–66.

Ueda, K., & Valencia, F. (2014). Central Bank Independence and Macroprudential Regulation. *Economic Letters, 125*(2), 327–330.

van der Waal, Z., & van Hout, E. T. (2009). Is Public Value Pluralism Paramount? The Intrinsic Multiplicity and Hybridity of Public Values. *International Journal of Public Administration Review, 32*(3–4), 220–231.

Varoufakis, Y. (2016). *And the Weak Suffer What They Must? Europe's Crisis and America's Future.* New York: Nation Books.

Walsh, C. E. (1995). Optimal Contracts for Central Bankers. *American Economic Review, 85*(1), 150–167.

Wang, S. (2016). *Examining the Effects of Dollarization on Ecuador.* Washington, DC: Council on Hemispheric Affairs.

Wanna, J., & Rhodes, R. (2007). The Limits to Public Value, or Rescuing Responsible Government from the Platonic Gardens. *Australian Journal of Public Administration, 66*(4), 406–421.

Waud, R. N. (1970). Public Interpretation of Federal Reserve Discount Rate Changes: Evidence on the" Announcement Effect". *Econometrica: Journal of the Econometric Society, 38*(2), 231–250.

Williams, I., & Shearer, H. (2011). Appraising Public Value: Past, Present and Futures. *Public Administration, 89*(4), 1367–1384.

Chapter 6

Conclusion

The kaleidoscope of public managers

For the purposes of presenting a concluding chapter, it is worth encapsulating the journey taken in earlier sections by first revisiting the ambition of this book as stated in its introductory section. At its core, the book sought to "reimagine the public manager" as an agent who is in fact more nuanced, more versatile, and richer than how she is traditionally portrayed in the Public Value (PV) literature. This would resonate with what van Hout and van der Waal termed the "multiplicity and hybridity" of PVT (2009), and would echo what Williams and Shearer admired about the nature of PVT as "an affirmation of managerial ingenuity and expertise" that would go "beyond policy implementation to the more proactive exercising of creativity and entrepreneurialism" (Williams & Shearer, 2011, p. 1372). In Moore's own words, PVT serves as "a framework that helps us connect what we believe is valuable and requires public resources, with improved ways of understanding what our 'publics' value, and how we connect to them" (Moore, 1995).

Yet the gap identified by this book was that PVT had proceeded without sufficiently theorizing about public managers and without sufficiently pondering who these agents really were. There was an insufficient definitional exploration of where the boundary lay between who is and isn't a "public manager," and how that delineation might take place. The reason for this gap, I suggested, was that PVT hadn't deconstructed the "public manager" since it has focused more on seeking case studies of *value,* in the sense of both articulating values and creating value. For example, in his very first exposition of PVT (Moore, 1994), the founder Mark Moore did not begin with any definition of the public manager. In fact, Moore began with the "what?" rather than the "who?" (1994, p. 296), and appears to have taken it for granted that his academic and practitioner audiences would be clear about who the protagonists of PVT were. As a result, in lieu of elaborating on who public managers are, he instead raised three other questions that were more pressing in his judgment: "What is the goal of public sector managers? What are they supposed to produce? And how will their performance be measured?" (1994, p. 296). Moore's early works themselves used seemingly synonymous lexical elements such as "public executive," "public sector manager," and "government managers" (1994, pp. 300–301).

This was in fact one of numerous ambiguities identified within the PVT literature by various scholars, since many important concepts within public value had been modified over time, but often subtly and without explicit enunciation, even by stalwarts such as its founder Moore (see analysis in Prebble, 2015). As Williams and Shearer remark, "the public value doctrine has been supplemented by newer interpretations and applications and, in the process, commentators (not least Moore himself) have reworked the themes and concepts involved" (2011, p. 1367). Morrell remarked that "further clarification, specification and consensus over concepts and terminology" is still wanting in the PV discourse (2009), and Stoker observed that there is a "lack of clarity of response" in terms of providing "plausible answers" to various aspects of PVT (Stoker, 2006, p. 49). Even scholars with a disposition favorable toward PVT expressed concerns about this yawning gap. For example, Williams and Shearer lamented that "there remains some lack of clarity over what public value is, both as a theory and as a descriptor of specific public actions and programmes" (2011, p. 1367), and they further observed that "the public value framework does not derive from a particular research tradition and there is, as yet, little by way of empirical research to support the claims made for it" (2011, p. 1381). As a result, PVT is aptly characterized either by a multiplicity of hybrid definitions (van der Waal & van Hout, 2009), or as an "umbrella concept that is still being typologized" (Alford & O'Flynn, 2009, p. 187), which is why it needs to be "rescued from ambiguity" (Prebble, 2012, p. 392).

My proposition in this book was to deploy those types of non-traditional public managers (NTMs) who had yet not been sufficiently explored, often because they did not fit neatly into context-independent categories of public managers (see Poocharoen, 2013), or because in the historical formation of Western, liberal governments (i.e. the general focus of PVT), these were not generally thought of as bureaucrats per se. The four NTMs that were chosen included: judicial officials (Chapter 2), armed forces officials (Chapter 3), public managers at multilateral institutions (International Monetary Fund (IMF), Chapter 4), and central bankers (Chapter 5). Each of these was given a PV-oriented treatment that had thus far remained wanting in the literature. On the one hand, this represented an infusion of novelty in PVT, but on the other hand and more importantly, it was also a test for what had been hailed as PVT's "non-didactic flexibility of application" (Williams & Shearer, 2011, p. 1374).

To put it in the language of public value, these NTMs offered "concrete managerial settings" (Meynhardt, 2009, p. 214) where public value could be examined, and could serve scholars with compelling studies to "structure thinking" about what ought to be the case, as well as to "diagnose the existing situation" (Meynhardt, 2009, p. 174). The explorations were envisaged as a twofold enterprise: first, they would help inform our understanding of who public managers might be in a broader sense; and second, PVT lenses would be used to contextualize the work of these institutions in a wider context. This reciprocal inquiry would thus enrich both the academic and practitioner perspectives, which supports William and Shearer's claim that "public value emerges as an approach that is rooted in everyday practice and retains a non-didactic flexibility of application" (2011, p. 1374). The chapters followed a propositional method, thereby exploring PVT-specific elements in a sequential manner across each of the NTMs. For three of the NTMs, the provenance of the propositions derived from the exploratory process of the chapters, but in one chapter (multilaterals/IMF), the propositions were derived from earlier work that studied the value creation of supranational entities (Chohan, 2019) and transposed them to the context of a global public. Through the propositional approach various PVT tools could be applied, most notably that of Moore's strategic triangle (Moore, 1994, 1995), which is the "central symbol" of public value (Alford & O'Flynn, 2009, p. 173).

Strategic triangle approaches

The elements of the triangle, namely, legitimacy, recognition of value, and operational resources, were each considered as part of the mutually reinforcing exploration that situated the NTMs within PVT and reciprocally offered insights from PVT for the NTMs. In the case of the **judiciary** (Chapter 2), the legitimacy element of the strategic triangle emphasized that judicial officials must be perceived as legitimate, independent, self-sufficient, nonpartisan, and responsible. Yet the independence of judiciaries was premised on nuances and qualifications in many countries, and legitimacy or independence does not alone or automatically translate into high degrees of value creation. Adding the node of value-recognition to legitimacy pointed out that different groups within the public may confer different levels of legitimacy and recognition, based on their historical and ongoing relationships with these public managerial institutions. Additionally, looking that operational resources of judiciaries highlighted the perennial shortage that they face, even as their requirements rise, including budgetary, legal, training, enforcement, case-management, and technological resources. At the same time, although the supply of justice remains somewhat fixed, the demand for justice continues to grow due to a variety of factors including population growth, litigiousness, and increased complexity in society. PVT's central symbol thus helps to present the public value case for judiciaries with clarity and simplicity.

In the case of the **armed forces** (Chapter 3), it was observed that they must be perceived as guardians of the public's security and defense, acting as legitimate, disciplined, and vigilant institutions. They may garner a greater recognition for their value proposition through both defense and non-defense means, such as by assisting civilian administration (particularly in disaster relief management). They must in essence cement their legitimacy and recognition through the process of co-creating values with other stakeholders for the public. If they do not, civil-military tensions might ensue that can erode their legitimacy. At the same time, with their possession of the legitimate use of violence, they can depose politicians and public managers through the use of force, which creates a tense public managerial dichotomy. From an operational resources perspective, it was noted that armed forces require a host of operating capabilities and resources, including budgetary, technical, weaponry, training, technological, physical, logistical, and material resources. Furthermore, the technological curve and the need to maintain consistent advantages mean that armed forces will always face limitations regardless of their operational endowment, and they must therefore aim to persistently optimize within constraints.

In the case of **multilaterals** (Chapter 4), particularly the IMF, it was noted that such institutions face a difficulty of legitimization in the eyes of citizens whenever the policies they impose cause undue public value destruction. Yet some politicians seek reciprocal legitimation with the IMF, using its recommendations to mete out policies that would otherwise be politically unfeasible. Meanwhile, the IMF garners legitimation for its role by presenting politicians with adjustment programs that will supposedly fix the economic problems that the public faces. Over time, however, if citizens do not recognize meaningful value creation, there is a loss of public trust in both national politicians and multilaterals. In terms of the recognition of their value, it was observed that there may be a divergence between the recognition of multilaterals in the short- and long-run. For example, in times of crisis, there may be a recognition of the value that the IMF can provide to stabilize financial systems and bail out governments. In the long-run, austerity and other reductions in social expenditures, which are important to citizens, may lead to a refusal to recognize the value in IMF propositions. At the same time, the transparency and accountability of the IMF's plans and workings are themselves a notable gap that perpetuates a declining recognition of its value proposition.

Additionally, in terms of discussing operational resources, it was suggested that countries that enter into IMF programs are forced to adhere to constraints and make "structural adjustments," which limit the operational resources available to national-level politicians and public managers for value creation. Their hands may be tied even on basic provisions of value to the public such as social protection. Politicians and national-level public managers may ultimately attempt to wrest back control of surrendered operational resources from multilateral institutions. From the perspective of the multilaterals themselves, a concern was raised that the major donor countries that support these institutions (notably the United States) are gradually withdrawing their commitments to these organizations, thereby limiting the operational wherewithal that they require to function effectively.

In the case of **central banks** (Chapter 5), it was remarked that across both developed and developing countries, these institutions have enjoyed various degrees of independence and of legitimacy. However, the space of economic neutrality, the reputation as technical experts, and the various forms of independence that central banks have enjoyed for many decades are increasingly coming into question, as politicians and citizens post-Global Financial Crisis (GFC) 2008 have demanded a fresh look into the value proposition of central banks as unelected officials spearheading monetary policy and financial supervision. In terms of the recognition of their public value, it was argued that each aspect of central bank value creation should be recognized separately for its contribution. In (developed country) monetary policy, inflation has been curbed, but unemployment and economic growth are increasing concerns. In financial supervision, central bank coordination has been forthcoming, but microprudential and macroprudential risks remain, and whether a single institution should take charge of financial supervision is still debatable. Additionally, the operational resources of central banks were framed in terms of their toolkits to resolve various parameters in monetary policy and financial supervision. In general, central bank operational resources are greater now than before the GFC, but there is a great deal of variety among countries. Operational resources might be constrained by the public's future choices to reduce Central Bank Independence (CBI).

The aim of summarizing the strategic triangle findings for each NTM in this section is to demonstrate the applicability of public value approaches to their function. The strategic triangle, having served on a great many occasions as a tool for public value analysis (see Chohan, 2017, 2019), has once again proven its utility in the cases of NTMs with such different scopes of function. Yet the inquiry of this book was not merely relegated to mechanical application of the strategic triangle to NTMs, but rather to also draw upon recent questions in public value where the perspectives of NTMs could inform these salient debates (see Chohan & Jacobs, 2017, 2018).

Recent questions in public value

Three questions that had emerged in recent years about PVT involved the nature of public value in the political sphere ("**public value in politics**"), the use of PVT as a rhetorical strategy to justify public managerial empowerment ("**public value and rhetoric**"), and the **destruction of public value**. Two of these were identified by Alford and O'Flynn (2009) as critiques that stood out which had yet to be either corroborated or refuted by meaningful discussions in the public value literature, while the third emerged from Spano's cautioning of political misallocations that would counter value-creating efforts (2009). Chohan and Jacobs (2017, 2018) gave both of these questions a precise treatment using the lens of legislative budget offices (LBOs). They found that rhetoric is indeed an existing PV gambit but not one exclusively relegated to public managers. In fact, *politicians* could also delve into rhetoric of value creation, in part because they (along with public managers) faced limiting constraints on their ability to address the multitude of conflicting and contradictory values that are articulated by the public (Chohan & Jacobs, 2018).

For public value in politics, Chohan and Jacobs challenged the notion of public managers as usurpers of democratic powers (as alleged by Wanna & Rhodes, 2007), by showing that specific types of public managers could straddle the politics–administration dichotomy (Roberts, 1995), therein enhancing both "efficiency" and "democracy" (see Stoker, 2006). This approach was revisited (Chohan, 2019), however, at the supranational level with European Union (EU) structures, and a contrasting result was presented in that the same institutions at the national level are likely to act differently than when imposed from above – a point that was relevant to the multilaterals examined in this book as well (see Chapter 4). For public value destruction, Chohan (2019) used the Congressional Budget Office's case study on US President Trump's 2017 attempt to repeal Obamacare as an example of public managers thwarting excessive public value destruction, pointing to the revocation of access to healthcare for 20 million citizens as a form of destruction that public managers could avert.

In this section, it is worth exploring the degree to which "public value in politics," "public value and rhetoric," and "public value destruction" were examined in this book through cases of different NTMs. Chapter 2 on the judiciary indicated that judicial officials enjoy a statutory independence from politicians that is often enshrined in constitutions or key national documents, thus reframing "public value in politics." Judges are thus not beholden to politicians as Moore's "final arbiters of value" (1995, p. 38) in well-functioning democratic societies, and in fact are expected to hold politicians to account in breaches of the law. At the same time, judiciaries can risk engaging in *judicial activism* and *judicial overreach* that would push them into the political sphere to a degree that would corroborate Wanna and Rhodes' fear of democratic usurpation (2007), and also lead to "public value destruction."

Chapter 3 on militaries explored the fact that militaries hold access to the legitimate use of violence as part of their mandate to provide security. The use of force could be diverted toward the usurpation of democratic mandates including the dissolution of assemblies and the imposition of martial law, which would exemplify (perhaps to the maximum degree) the notion of "public value in politics" as an infringement on democracy. "Public value in rhetoric" would apply in this instance if militaries told the public that they were only assuming the reins of power temporarily and would restore civilian rule "in due course." If they continued to maintain their hold on power against the broader wishes and values of the public, then they would risk fomenting public value destruction, particularly if civil society rose up to challenge military NTMs.

Chapter 4 on multilaterals examined public value in politics similarly to Chohan's (2019) study of supranational public managers extracting power from national politicians. It argued that there was a surrender of operational resources from national-level politicians and public managers to multilateral public managers, which would then override national democratic mandates. Chapter 4 argued that the IMF represented a rather brute and evident form of "public value in politics." The chapter also considered "public value and rhetoric" by drawing the distinction between the praxis of the IMF's structural adjustment programs from the benign rhetoric of "a cooperative of 185 member countries, whose objective is to promote world economic stability and growth" (Fritz-Krockow & Ramlogan, 2007, p. 1). The aspect of value destruction was covered extensively in Chapter 4, indicating that the destructive element could be highlighted regardless of the approach of analysis, whether focusing on civil riots, austerity measures, eroding social protections, or various other aspects that destroy value for national-level publics.

Chapter 5 on central banks examined "public value in politics" very carefully because of the nature of central bank independence (CBI), which set these NTMs at a distance from direct political intrusion, at least in the sphere of monetary policy (but not financial supervision). Goal independence, functional independence, and institutional independence represented various forms of CBI that had grown as an international model in the late 20th century, but which has been revisited after the 2008 GFC, in part because of the public's perception of central bank culpability in that crisis, but also because the aim of CBI in curbing inflation seems to be a more remote and less relevant phenomenon in industrialized societies. The discussion of Chapter 5 suggested that CBI would likely decline across many countries in the coming years.

In terms of "public value and rhetoric," the chapter's insight was twofold. First, the usage of technical jargon in the complex domain of monetary policy is employed by central banks to keep political overseers at bay. Second, and more enriching, was the observation that central banks use rhetoric as a means to signal their future expectations about the economy, but this is influential enough to direct the expectations of the public itself. In other words, rhetoric is not just a vehicle for public managers to react to values articulated by citizens (Chohan & Jacobs, 2018), but can actually shape the values held by citizens. Finally, the chapter also highlighted the influence that central banks exerted on policies that culminated in the 2008 GFC, which makes them a party to the public value destruction of the financial crisis, and they must now face a public that is increasingly wary of granting them the same level of institutional and functional independence as before.

Lessons for NTMs

Interplay between NTMs

The NTMs of this book would, at first glance, appear to have little in common: judges, generals, IMF staff, and central bankers. Yet, they form part of the larger architecture of public administration, and manifest interesting

Conclusion 121

connections across their fields of engagement. In other words, they are not disembodied public manager entities, but rather serve as co-interacting agents in the public value-creation processes of society (Table 6.1).

For the **judiciary**, it is important to observe that the justice system is inherently entwined with most (if not all) aspects of socio-managerial life. For example, it was noted in Chapter 2 through the example of the Lawyer's Movement (Ahsan, 2009) that they could challenge military rule. Judiciaries can also rule against multilateral institutions operating in their jurisdictions. In addition, they can also serve an important role along with central banks in financial supervision (see Restoy, 2018). For the **military**, the interplay with other NTMs might appear less evident, but the Lawyer's Movement

Table 6.1 Examples of interplay between NTMs

Agency	Domain			
	Judiciary	Military	Multilaterals	Central Bankers
Judiciary		The lawyers movement to challenge military rule (e.g. Pakistan; see Ahsan, 2009)	Litigation involving the IMF, WB, UN and other multilaterals in their jurisdictions	Financial supervision falls both institutions (see Restoy, 2018)
Military	Appointment of judges sympathetic to military rule (e.g. Pakistan; see Ahsan, 2009)		UN Peacekeeping missions (see Peter, 2019)	
Multilaterals	Int'l Court of Justice, other judicial & arbitration mechanisms (e.g. WTO)	NATO and other joint defense & security arrangements (Jakobsen, 2018)		IMF pushes for central bank independence (Kern et al., 2019)
Central Bankers	Central banks pursuing the resolution of troubled entities (Restoy, 2018)		Fed now acts as another "global lender of last resort" (Broz, 2015)	

Source: Author's research; Ahsan (2009), Broz (2015), Restoy (2018), Jakobsen (2018), Peter (2019), Kern et al. (2019).

is suggestive of how judges might be favorably appointed during episodes of military rule (Ahsan, 2009). Chapter 3 mentioned an interesting form of multilateral engagement through the notion of collective security, where UN peacekeeping missions (Peter, 2019) and North Atlantic Treaty Organization (NATO) (Jakobsen, 2018) illustrate military engagement in multilateral arrangements.

For **multilaterals** and international civil servants, it is important to note that international agreements have led to the creation of multilateral institutions in a great variety of domains. In the judicial sense, the International Court of Justice and other arbitration bodies (such as the World Trade Organization (WTO)) serve specific justice-oriented purposes. In the military sense, the aforementioned NATO and UN Peacekeeping arrangements (Jakobsen, 2018; Peter, 2019) offer ample evidence of multilateral collaboration. For central banks, it was noted in Chapter 5 that the IMF pushes for central bank independence (CBI) as a mechanism for ensuring the apolitical execution of its recommendations (Kern et al., 2019). For **central banks**, one form of interplay with the judiciary was observed in the "resolution of troubled entities" to minimize systemic risk (Restoy, 2018). To compare central banks with multilateral organizations such as the IMF, it was observed in Chapter 5 that the Federal Reserve acts as another form of "lender of last resort" during crises such as the GFC of 2008–2009 (Broz, 2015).

As such, the interplay between the NTMs chosen in this book illustrates how agents can co-create value across multiple domains beyond what might be their traditionally conceived remit. Usually, PVT's emphasis is on co-creation between three agents, but it is time to examine co-creation among public managers themselves. Further research must delve into the points of public managerial interplay through the lens of public value, which would bolster Moore's assertion of co-creating value across the cadres of society (1995).

Macro-micro

The discussion of Chapter 5 illustrated the question of producing value at the micro and macro levels, specifically regarding the microprudential and macroprudential aspects of central bank value creation, wherein Goodhart et al. sought to explore what kind of "perspective supervisors in different institutional settings may adopt: a macro-oriented perspective or a more micro-approach" (2002, p. 398). In this concluding chapter, a similar micro–macro distinction can be applied to all of the NTMs of this book, along with a mention of which is given greater emphasis by each NTM. Table 6.2 enumerates applications of macro-micro public value approaches for each of the non-traditional managers considered in this book.

In the case of each NTM, the methods and implications are somewhat different. For **central banks**, microprudential and macroprudential distinctions (Restoy, 2018), as the difference between specific vulnerabilities and

Table 6.2 Macro and micro perspectives on value creation

NTM	Micro-level Focus	Macro-level Focus	General Current Tilt	Maximum Public Value
Judiciary	Address fairness in each case & deliberation. But: this means case backlog can swell.	Emphasize performance and efficiency in overall judicial system. But: due attention to fairness and nuance of each case might be overlooked.	Micro.	Balancing both fairness and efficiency – ensuring a quality of justice but also a quantity.
Military	Address specific threats from groups, individuals, or movements, as in preemption of attacks or events.	Address broader security threats, with geopolitical or national/regional interests and their shifts in mind.	Not generalizable – some prioritize micro challenges, while others stress macro-focus.	Managing both wider geopolitical challenges as well as specific local threats to assure comprehensive security.
Multilateral (IMF)	Address economic reforms in specific countries with adjustment programs or reform packages.	Address global monetary stability and avoiding crisis contagion while keeping the overall financial architecture in mind.	Macro – even at the expense of individual (developing) countries.	Ensure global monetary stability & circulation while avoiding the worsening of distress in struggling developing countries.
Central Banks	Attain micro-targets such as stable inflation and unemployment through micro-tools like interest rates. Microprudential oversight.	Attain macro-level targets such as mitigation of banking crisis risks; assessing levels of overall liquidity, lending, and stability. Macroprudential oversight.	Macro – greater stabilization and supervisory roles than in the past. Also, micro-tools are limited today (zero-level interest rates).	Ensure overall banking system stability, stable currency, reasonable inflation, & employment, while working with other public managers & politicians.

Source: Author's research.

overall financial stability, are a useful separation to instill. A similar logic can be applied to **multilaterals** such as the IMF, where micro-interventions include assistance to specific countries, while macro-interventions include the contagion of regional or global economic crises (Dresner, 2012). In the case of central banks and multilaterals, the tilt has been toward macro-approaches, given that the fallout of international economic contagion is multiplicative and can spread quickly when the overall system is destabilized or in panic (Greenspan, 2013). For the **military**, the micro-approach involves the mitigation of specific threats, while the macro approach involves assuring an overall deterrence and general level of security. It is difficult to generalize on whether militaries emphasize the macro or micro given the context-specific nature of armed forces' decision-making that leads to interdependent notions of security: sufficient control over micro risks leads to better macro outcomes, and vice versa. However, as critical social theorists note, the concept of violence is "largely ignored in public administration, a field in which people concentrate on micro implementation rather than macro societal context and often avoid questioning oppressive or inequitable structures and practices" (Box, 2015, p. 4). Finally, for **judicial** officials, it is the micro-level attention to each case that receives emphasis in most justice systems, even though the highest judicial performance is evidently found where macro considerations about the overall process's efficiency and fairness are both given due weight (Palumbo et al., 2013).

These examinations suggest that there is a useful analytical distinction to be made in evaluating the stance of public managerial institutions in terms of their emphasis on micro- or macro-approaches to value creation. Future research must take this line of inquiry forward, emphasizing particularly how such institutions might diverge between countries, or at the national vs. subnational level. For example, drawing upon the public value work on legislative budget offices (LBOs, see Chohan & Jacobs, 2017, 2018; Chohan, 2019), an argument may be made for macro-level value creation in certain LBOs such as the Congressional Budget Office (CBO), but for micro-level emphasis on local costing at the Australian Parliamentary Budget Office (PBO).

Outfield value

Public managers are generally appointed to fulfill specific value-creating mandates. However, their ambitions and scope may be diluted or expanded over time due to a variety of factors. By that account, we may apply the term *outfield value* to describe what occurs when public managers seek to create value in domains outside of their specialization. To some extent, such efforts can be successful, if they cohere with the overarching purpose of the institution itself. For example, an air force which provides a comprehensive and multifaceted training to its officers can enable them to contribute to value creation outside the air force itself (see Pakistani example in Chapter 2).

However, this book has highlighted far more cases that backfire when public managers attempt outfield value creation. Chapter 2 drew upon an example of judicial overreach when a Chief Justice sought to raise funds for building dams and fell short by 99.4%, and yet the justice threatened that critics of the dam funds could be tried for treason. Indeed, it is dubious whether judicial public managers are best equipped to engage in crowdfunding activities. Chapter 3 drew upon the example of militaries engaging in real estate, while Chapter 4 considered the imposition of IMF policies that went beyond direct macroeconomic stabilization and affected society more broadly, which would lead to public value destruction in many instances. Meanwhile, in drawing upon the work of Goodhart et al. (2002), Chapter 5 highlighted that over-engaging economists rather than lawyers as public managers in the banking-supervisory arms of central banks would have consequences for stability of the banking system. Table 6.3 briefly enumerates these points.

What may be inferred from these examples of outfield value is that public managers must contend with the risk of public value destruction if they extend themselves too far beyond their mandates. This has been suggested on multiple occasions in the public administration literature more broadly (see PV example in Wanna & Rhodes, 2007). However, this notion of outfield value requires a more deliberate examination in PVT, and not just for the NTMs studied in this book. Outfield value constitutes a concept akin to the non-traditional manager, in that it seeks to delineate what is valuable from what is not, in the same way that NTMs draw distinctions between those agents that represent public managers and those that do not. Future research must therefore proactively consider examples of outfield value, both successful and otherwise.

Table 6.3 Unsuccessful attempts at outfield value creation

NTM	Examples of Unsuccessful Attempts at Outfield Value Creation
Judiciary	Activities in the fiscal realm such as fundraising from civil society sources (e.g. raising funds for large projects from civil society sources)
Military	Engagements in market-based activities (real estate, property development)
Multilateral	Impositions on structural factors in developing countries which decimate social expenditures (IMF programs in numerous developing countries)
Central Banks	Hiring excesses of economists instead of lawyers and other experts in the banking-supervisory roles (OECD countries pre-2008 crisis)

Source: Author's research; discussions in preceding chapters.

Politics-administration dichotomy

The politics–administration dichotomy (Roberts, 1995; Chohan, 2017) represents a dynamic that has emerged throughout the explorations of this book and in a particularly interesting sense: in each case, the general assumption or consensus has been that the NTMs had left the dichotomy settled in their favor, or in a manner that politics would not intercede too much in their value-creation exercise without some significant trade-offs. Going through the list, this seems to be a recurrent theme: judiciaries should be independent branches of government; central banks should conduct monetary policy without political predilections; multilateral institutions should avoid excess politicization to create a cooperative international system where value creation is possible; and militaries should not step into politics unless there is a breakdown of civil administration or other extreme circumstance (Table 6.4).

Yet despite the assumption that the arguments for de-politicizing these NTMs would be clear-cut, in praxis their independence as public managers appears to be shifting around the world due to various underlying forces. For judiciaries, particularly in the developing world, many governments are challenging the independence of judiciaries and making them subservient to executive rule. For militaries, the presence of dictatorships and martial law in various zones of the world suggests that civilian rule has yet to entrench itself. Future research must engage with questions raised in this book about militaries, including the concept of PV destruction as PV creation, and the PV for the wider international public through multinational security. For multilateral organizations (e.g. IMF), the subversion of these institutions to the interests of a select few means that they are used as instruments to oppose

Table 6.4 Politics-administration dichotomy: assumptions for each NTM

NTM	Assumptions
Judiciary	Well-functioning judiciaries that are constitutionally independent can operate as a check on other branches of government.
Military	Militaries have access to the legitimate use of violence, but should only step in to assist civilian administration and not interfere in civilian politics unless a degree of administrative breakdown has already occurred.
Multilateral	Multilaterals are more effective at creating value for the world-public if they were not excessively politicized by a handful of powerful nations.
Central Banks	Goal, functional, and institutional independence are forms of CBI that are perceived to be most effective at controlling macroeconomic variables (e.g. inflation) when politicians do not interfere in the space.

Source: Author's research; discussions in preceding chapters.

national-level political and public managerial value creation. For central banks, the track record of the GFC 2008 has led civil society and politicians to question whether central banks truly deserve such sweeping powers in the monetary domain. What these examples show is that the politics-administration dichotomy is filled with greater nuances and with finer perspectives when seen through cases of NTMs.

Limitations

This book set out on an unusual path within PVT and thus reaped the benefits of a distinctive approach to the study of value creation. However, this approach also brought with it certain hefty drawbacks, which future research must seek to address. As a first point, the book did not help to address the gap in PVT on empirical approaches (see Williams & Shearer, 2011, p. 1374). The propositional method pursued in each chapter offered a creative exploration of value-creating processes, but as a downside, the use of the propositional method perpetuates what Williams and Shearer observe about "the risk that public value fails to develop a secure empirical foundation and loses clarity and distinctiveness as an approach to practice" (2011, p. 1374).

While there is nothing inherently inferior about the correct application of non-empirical methods, the critique of PVT as lacking a "secure empirical foundation" continues to linger. That said, this book did address another (harsher) critique of PVT along the same lines, which was that PV has become a "Humpty Dumpty term [that is] both everywhere and nowhere" (Oakley et al., 2006, p. 2; see also Crabtree, 2004), because it "seems to be a messy hybrid of [public goods, public interest, and public domain] – without any of their history or intellectual robustness" (Oakley et al., 2006, p. 3). The concept of public goods was given a clearer grounding in PVT through this book through explorations of defense (Chapter 3), multilaterals (Chapter 4), and central banks (Chapter 5), which should put harsher critics of PVT at some ease, even as greater theorization is still required to put the matter to rest.

As a second point, a foreseeable critique of the book's analysis may regard the specific choice of NTMs: why judiciaries, militaries, multilaterals, or central banks? As the earlier section on the interplay between NTMs illustrates, the choice of public managers can be an important determinant in answering recent questions that have emerged in PVT (e.g. rhetoric, politics, destruction). But these might be answered by other NTMs, who may also demonstrate a degree of interplay and connection with the questions raised earlier. The best answer is that these NTMs were, in my judgment, the most suitable in "reimagining the public manager," because of the nuances that undergird their work, and the peculiar nature of the value-creation processes they undertake in concert with other agents in society. They are, however, by no means the only NTMs who could contribute to the PVT literature. In fact, the list can be quite long if given to enumeration, and the field remains open for the selection of numerous other NTMs, in part because the PVT is "umbrella concept that is still being typologized" (Alford & O'Flynn, 2009, p. 187), but also because of the inherent divergences between who is and isn't considered a public manager in each society (Poocharoen, 2013).

A few suggestions for future researchers may be offered at this juncture. First, diplomats offer an interesting lens because of the nature of their PV creation between and across national boundaries. They create value not only for their own public but also for the public to which they act as emissaries, and they respond to the values both of their original public as well as that where they carry a sovereign mission. In my judgment, diplomats would offer a fascinating exploration of NTM value-creation for an international public. In addition, similarly to central banks (Chapter 5), State-Owned Enterprises (SOEs), Public-Private Partnerships (PPPs), and Sovereign Wealth Funds (SWFs) offer interesting examples of value co-creation wherein public managers must engage with a market logic. The market (and private interest more broadly) is something of a blind-spot in PVT (Benington, 2009; Chohan, 2019), and so must be more readily addressed. As a final suggested example, autonomous bodies represent another form of NTM that create value for specific domains where excessive market intrusion of politicization is likely. These bodies are established in a variety of domains, including strategic resources, the fine arts, historical preservation (museums), and religious praxis. The exploration of each or any of these might enrich our understandings of public managers.

As a third point, a choice had to be made between *depth* and *breadth* in this book. Breadth would have allowed for an exploration of some NTMs noted in the previous point, but then the relevant depth of exploration could not have been achieved (see CBI in Chapter 5 as a good example). The fundamental issue lies in achieving the requisite level of familiarity with each NTM's original literature, which is an absolute *must* for scholars to be able to situate their public value contributions in a lucid manner. Put another way, each public manager must be understood within their own literature, which is often vast and highly developed. After all, there is a long tradition in jurisprudence in many different cultures that inform the workings of judicial officials, just as there is a vast literature on central banks and monetary policy which has flourished in the past century. The same applies to war studies for the armed forces, and for international political economy (and development studies) to multilaterals. This was perhaps the greatest challenge in producing this volume, given that a familiarity with the literature of each NTM had to be attained and thoroughly understood to then situate their praxis in PVT. As such, far more questions remain about the nuances around public managers than could be answered in one volume, but this opens the field for future PV scholars to explore proactively and enthusiastically.

As a fourth point, given the nature of PVT exploration undertaken in this book and the requirement for treating new types of public managers, the book was pushed toward the introduction of new terminology. This has been a point of contention in PVT for quite some time, as when Morrell remarks that "further clarification, specification and consensus over concepts and terminology" is still wanting in the PV discourse (2009), and Stoker observes that there is a "lack of clarity of response" in terms of providing "plausible answers" to various aspects of PVT (Stoker, 2006, p. 49). In fact, many terms have quietly changed their connotations (see analysis in Prebble, 2015). While scholarship in the social sciences and humanities is somewhat averse to the frivolous introduction of new terms, this book truly required a broadening of the lexicon regarding PVT concepts. Non-traditional manager (NTM) is perhaps the most evident example of this, but so are concepts such as *outfield value* (see earlier section). It is questionable whether such terms are likely to stick in the PV discourse, but they do serve an important purpose within the illustration of value-creating processes in this book, and may come to assist the inquiry of other scholars in the years to come.

As a fifth point, this book sought to draw examples from around the world in the contexts of both developed and developing countries. This approach was inspired by the concern that developing country contexts have not received sufficient treatment in the PV literature (see Samaratunge & Wijewardena, 2009; Samaratunge & Pillay, 2011). The limitation that is worth mentioning here is that the public managerial experience differs substantially between developed countries and developing countries; and therefore, when this book drew focus on developing country contexts (e.g. judiciary, armed forces, multilaterals), its applicability was inadvertently limited for developed countries, as, for example, regarding concerns about martial law. Conversely, the emphasis on developed country contexts in certain chapters (e.g. central banks) detracted from their relevance to developing country cases, as, for example, regarding persistently low inflation. Although an effort was made to strike the appropriate balance (judicial performance would be a good example), there was invariably some degree of trade-off which had to be accepted in the experiences of national publics based on their levels of socioeconomic development. In hindsight, a specific volume on NTMs in developing countries might have drawn better attention to the impediments to value creation, and future research should be encouraged to explore developing country contexts in their rightful exclusivity.

As a sixth point, some traditionally-minded PV theorists might express dissatisfaction with the lack of treatment of the usually chosen public managerial institutions, such as in healthcare, taxation, education, and law enforcement. I am inclined to pay this critique short shrift, because it is almost tautological and self-evident that out-of-the-box approaches are only likely to yield fruit if they are truly outside of PVT's usual "box." My vision for PVT entails its application to a broader frontier of social agents, and this requires looking beyond the stagnating trend that has come befall PVT's case studies. The theory is simply too young to fall pretty to an old guard of theorists who would pose as its *eminences grises* looking at the usual managerial-types. The approach that this book has advocated recommends expanding PVT to promising new horizons by first revisiting its first principles. The very protagonist of PVT is what has been questioned here through multiple NTMs, and I believe that similar revisitations of PV's essential terms are in order.

Reimagining the public managers

After all of the exploration of NTMs undertaken in this book, students and adherents of public value theory should come away with the recognition that PVT is still an "umbrella concept that is still being typologized" (Alford & O'Flynn, 2009, p. 187), and which does need to be "rescued from ambiguity" (Prebble, 2012, p. 392), beginning with the recognition that the "public manager" of PVT is an agent more diverse and versatile than that for which she is given credit. Judicial officials, officers of the armed forces, staff at multilateral institutions, and central bankers are but some examples of public managers who had heretofore not received treatment through a PVT lens, but they are scarcely the only ones left for PV theorists to explore. In the deconstruction of public managerial institutions through PVT lenses, it is also public value itself that is being enriched as a literature. Far more questions remain about the nuances around public managers than could be answered in one volume, but the precedent has been set for more interdisciplinary and interconnected studies of public managers.

The continuation of future explorations of NTMs, along the lines of those conducted in this book, remains a deserving enterprise. It is an exercise in imagination and (re)discovery. None of the NTMs is particularly new, with judges and military officials existing far back in antiquity, central banks spanning 400 years, and multilaterals only being comparatively new since they are nearly a century old. But their superimposition into the PVT literature is a new exercise and certainly a timely one. Without bolder excursions toward the boundary of public managerial definitions, the theory risks a gradual stagnation interspersed with spurts of mild academic interest. At present, I lament to put it so frankly in that I observe much of the PV-oriented scholarship in leading academic journals to be of a tepid nature: gathering results from a hospital here, interviewing local government bureaucrats there; measuring utility company outputs here, and commenting on public broadcasting there. This is not the energetic pace that PVT deserves, and nor does this do justice to the original promise of framing public administrators as agents of value creation and co-creation. Just as the application of PV frameworks to NTMs goes to demonstrate, there are powerful perspectives to be gleaned through use of PV lenses in the praxis of public administration, which might not be arrived at through other theories in the field.

My final recommendation to students of PVT is to urge them to channel their own "value-seeking imagination" toward theoretical and practitioner explorations of the agents that strive to improve society. It is up to us, as a community of scholars, to resist the tendency in PVT toward ossification and perfunctory analyses that dissipate the necessary energies required to remold society though a finer architecture that (1) responds best to the values articulated by citizens, and (2) serves to create, sustain, and provide value to all members of the wider public. Continued studies of public managers by keen scholars would be instrumental toward that endeavor – *whomsoever they may be.*

References

Ahsan, A. (2009). The Preservation of the Rule of Law in Times of Strife. *International Law, 43*(1), 73–78.
Alford, J., & O'Flynn, J. (2009). Making Sense of Public Value: Concepts, Critiques and Emergent Meanings. *International Journal of Public Administration, 32*(3–4), 171–191.
Benington, J. (2009). Creating the Public in Order to Create Public Value? *International Journal of Public Administration, 32*(3–4), 232–249.
Box, R. C. (2015). *Critical Social Theory in Public Administration*. London: Routledge.
Broz, J. L. (2015). The Politics of Rescuing the World's Financial System: The Federal Reserve as a Global Lender of Last Resort. *Korean Journal of International Studies, 13*(2), 323–351.
Chohan, U. W. (2017). Independent Budget Offices and the Politics–Administration Dichotomy. *International Journal of Public Administration, 41*(12), 1009–1017.
Chohan, U. W. (2019). *Public Value and Budgeting: International Perspectives*. London: Routledge.
Chohan, U. W., & Jacobs, K. (2017). Public Value in Politics: A Legislative Budget Office Approach. *International Journal of Public Administration, 40*(12), 1063–1073. doi: 10.1080/01900692.2016.1242612
Chohan, U. W., & Jacobs, K. (2018). Public Value as Rhetoric: A Budgeting Approach. *International Journal of Public Administration, 41*(15), 1217–1227.
Crabtree, J. (2004). The Revolution That Started in a Library. *The New Statesman, 17*(826), 54–56.
Dresner, D. (2012). The Irony of Global Economic Governance: The System Worked. *Tufts University Papers: Fletcher School of Law & Diplomacy.*
Fritz-Krockow, B., & Ramlogan, P. (2007). *International Monetary Fund Handbook: Functions, Policies, and Operations.* Washington, DC: IMF.
Goodhart, C., Schoenmaker, D., & Dasgupta, P. (2002). The Skill Profile of Central Bankers and Supervisors. *Review of Finance, 6*(3), 397–427.
Greenspan, A. (2013). *The Map and the Territory: Risk, Human Nature, and the Future of Forecasting.* New York: Penguin.
Jakobsen, J. (2018). Is European NATO Really Free-riding? Patterns of Material and Non-Material Burden-Sharing after the Cold War. *European Security, 27*(4), 490–514.
Kern, A., Reinsberg, B., & Rau-Göhring, M. (2019). IMF Conditionality and Central Bank Independence. *European Journal of Political Economy, 59*(1), 212–229.
Meynhardt, T. (2009). Public Value Inside: What is Public Value Creation? *International Journal of Public Administration, 32*(3/4), 192–219.

Moore, M. (1994). Public Value as the Focus of Strategy. *Australian Journal of Public Administration, 53*(3), 296–303.

Moore, M. (1995). *Creating Public Value: Strategic Management in Government*. Cambridge, MA: Harvard University Press.

Morrell, K. (2009). Governance and the Public Good. *Public Administration, 87*(3), 538–556.

Oakley, K., Naylor, R., & Lee, D. (2006). *Giving Them What They Want: Constructing the 'Public' in Public Value*. London: BOP Consulting.

Palumbo, G., Giupponi, G., Nunziata, L., & Mora-Sanguinetti, J. (2013). *Judicial Performance and Its Determinants: A Cross-country Perspective*. Paris: OECD:

Peter, M. (2019). *Peacekeeping: Resilience of an Idea*. Cham: Palgrave Macmillan.

Poocharoen, O. (2013). Bureaucracy and the Policy Process. In E. F. Araral, S., M. Howlett, M. Ramesh, & X. Wu (Eds.), *Routledge Handbook of Public Policy* (p. 349–364). London: Routledge.

Prebble, M. (2012). Public Value and the Ideal State: Rescuing Public Value from Ambiguity. *Australian Journal of Political Administration, 71*(4), 392–402.

Prebble, M. (2015). Public Value and the Limits to Collaboration. *International Journal of Public Administration, 38*(7), 473–485.

Restoy, F. (2018). *Central Banks and Financial Oversight*. Paper presented at the Fundación Ramón Areces, Madrid.

Roberts, A. (1995). "Civic Discovery" as a Rhetorical Strategy. *Journal of Public Policy Analysis and Management, 14*(2), 291–307.

Samaratunge, R., & Pillay, S. (2011). Governance in Developing Countries: Sri Lanka and South Africa Compared. *International Journal of Public Administration, 34*(6), 389–398.

Samaratunge, R., & Wijewardena, N. (2009). The Changing Nature of Public Value in Developing Countries. *International Journal of Public Administration, 32*(3–4), 313–327.

Spano, A. (2009). Public Value Creation and Management Control Systems. *International Journal of Public Administration, 32*(3–4), 328–348.

Stoker, G. (2006). Public Value Management: A New Narrative for Networked Governance?. *American Review of Public Administration, 36*(1), 41–57.

van der Waal, Z., & van Hout, E. T. (2009). Is Public Value Pluralism Paramount? The Intrinsic Multiplicity and Hybridity of Public Values. *International Journal of Public Administration Review, 32*(3–4), 220–231.

Wanna, J., & Rhodes, R. (2007). The Limits to Public Value, or Rescuing Responsible Government from the Platonic Gardens. *Australian Journal of Public Administration, 66*(4), 406–421.

Williams, I., & Shearer, H. (2011). Appraising Public Value: Past, Present and Futures. *Public Administration, 89*(4), 1367–1384.

Index

Argentina 62, 70, 73–76, 80
armed forces: legitimacy 53–55; in non-defence roles 46–50; as public managers 50–53; spinoffs 47–49
Asian Infrastructure Investment Bank 79, 81, 84
Askari 49
attitude theory 18
austerity 66, 69, 75, 117, 120

Bank of England 90
Bank of France 90
Bretton Woods 79, 81
BRICS Bank 79, 84

case flow management 23, 28
CENTO 45
central bank independence 93–98
Chaudary, I. 31
creative power 46
critical social theorists 46–47

defence *see* security
defence forces *see* armed forces
Department of Defence 48

Eurogroup 62
European Central Bank 62, 89
European Union 23, 45, 61–62, 119
exchange rate policy 91

fact pattern theory 18
FATF 46, 61, 63
Fauji *see* Askari
Federal Reserve 88, 95–98, 102–103, 107–108

Global Financial Crisis 88–92, 97–98, 101–102, 118, 120
Global South 62
Graeber, D. 42, 47, 100, 109
Greece 76
Greenspan, A. 96, 101–102, 107

helicopter money 102

IMF: justifications 65–66; legitimacy 71–74; operational resources 76–78; as public managers 64–67
India: judiciary 24–25, 35; martial law 52, 54–55
interest rate policy 91, 104
Iraq 53

Japan 34
judicial performance 21–26
jurisprudence 18
justice system 18–20; approval rating 31, and Moore, M. 20

macro-micro approaches 122–124
macroprudential 91–92, 101, 118, 122–123
market integrity 91–93
martial law 41, 52–55
microprudential *see* macroprudential
military *see* armed forces

NATO 45
neoliberalism 47, 62, 65, 80
New Deal 19
New Zealand: neoliberalism 62; Reserve Bank 94

Nisar, S. 31–32
non-bank financial institutions 91–92
Non-Traditional Managers (NTMs) 5–8; Descriptions 11–14; lessons 120; interplay 120–127

OECD 21–22
One Belt One Road 81
organization theory 18
outfield value 124–125

Pakistan: Air Force 48, 124; Judicial activism 29–32; judicial overreach 29–32; military 51–52; peacekeeping 45, 51
Peoples Liberation Army 48
politics-administration dichotomy: in central banks 93; in judiciary 29; in military 53–55
presidentialisation thesis 97
public good *see* security
public-private partnerships 128

quantitative easing 100, 104

reciprocal legitimation 71
regulatory arbitrage 99
rhetoric: central banks 106–108; IMF 79–80
Rhodesia 34
role theory 18

SEATO 45
Security 43–47; aerial defence 43; collective security 45–47; as public good 43–45
separation of powers 19
social protection 69, 117, 120
sovereign wealth fund 128
strategic triangle: in central banks 100–105; in judiciary 26–29; in military 50–53; in multilateral context 71–77
structural adjustment programs 68, 72, 76, 82, 117
supply-side constraints 33

Taliban 21
technological curve 56
trial length 22–23

United Nations 45
United States: central bank (*see* Federal Reserve); Congressional Budget Office 119, 124; with IMF 77; military 51
University of New South Wales 48

value destruction: by militaries 45–48; by multilaterals 81
Varoufakis, Y. 62

weltgemeinschaft 63
World Bank 61–63, 66, 77–78
World Justice Project 24–26
World Trade Organization 122

zero-bound interest rates 104